For Nature, Not Humans

- Recollections of Brownsea Island under the ownership of Mrs Bonham Christie.

Collected and edited by Peter Moore

POOLE HISTORICAL TRUST
2003

This volume is published by the Poole Historical Trust whose primary aims are the promotion of research into and the publication of works on the history and life of Poole and the surrounding area.

Previous Publications

The Pride of Poole, 1688-1851

An Album of Old Poole

Mansions and Merchants of Poole and Dorset

Brownsea Islander

Poole and World War II

A Portfolio of Old Poole

Ebb-Tide at Poole

History of the Town of Poole, 1839 (reprint)

The Sydenhams of Poole (booklet)

Art in Poole and Dorset

Victorian Poole

Poole after World War II 1945-1953

D-Day Poole (booklet)

The Spirit of Poole 1953-1963

Lifeboatmen Never Turn Back

Schools of Old Poole

Poole's Pride Regained 1964-1974

Poole Was My Oyster

ISBN 187353545-7

Prepared for publication by Ian Andrews.
Designed by Andrew S Arnold.
Production by Graphic Editions, Poole.
Printed and bound in Great Britain by The Baskerville Press, Salisbury, Wiltshire.

CONTENTS

LIST OF ILLUSTRATIONS

INTRODUCTION

Mrs Mary Florence Christie (née Whitburn) purchased Brownsea Island in 1927. She lived there, even during World War II, until she died in 1961. She bought Brownsea Island as a reserve for wild life – not to be hunted and shot as in many country estates but as a true sanctuary for them. In a time when there was a world economic slump it was the more surprising that she was not expecting any return on the £125,000 (or thereabouts) she was paying for the Island. She did not manage the Island reserve but let nature take its course.

From the census records the population of the Island had reached 270 (Theophilus Bennett, Vicar, 1881), and she reduced the population to less than 10 people – at times to two and herself.

This book explores the background of Mrs Bonham Christie, the essential features of the development of the Island prior to 1927, the problems of the islanders from 1927 and the reactions to this novel idea of a natural wild life sanctuary. The inhabitants of Poole also had their entry restricted instead of freedom to land on the Island. Research has shown that a limited number were, however, allowed on the Island. During World War II Mrs Christie did not welcome the Army and Navy personnel sent to defend the Island and the entrance to Poole Harbour.

Barry Guest comments, 'You have to be a bit eccentric to want to live on an island like this'. Mrs Bonham Christie as an eccentric recluse generated many stories in the press, not all based on fact. Even in those days newspapers were likely to exaggerate even if the story had only a grain of truth! I am grateful for the information given me - often events remembered for 50 years or stories retold by relatives. I am grateful to those who were interested in the history of the Island who have recorded interviews or collected information over the last 40 years. Other than those evicted from the Island or their relatives, all have spoken with great affection for the Island and with some admiration of her efforts to create, almost single handedly, an Island nature reserve.

Poole Quay, on the mainland is a mere 2½ miles away. However Mrs Bonham Christie managed to detach herself from the changing lifestyles and pressures, living for 96 years, in spite of frugal conditions and diet. The plaque in St Mary's Church on Brownsea Island has the years 1863 – 1961. However she died in her 96th year. The memorial on the family vault at Marston Bigot churchyard correctly states:

Born 23rd July 1865

Died 8th April 1961

She was known as Mrs Bonham Christie or Mrs Christie. The Bonham is part of her husband's Christian names. The first person to be registered with a surname Bonham-Christie, with the hyphen was Robert, her great grandson. The Bonham and the Christie names have no connections with the auction houses and no connection with other families with Bonham in the surname.

Mrs Bonham Christie in the early 1900's.

MRS BONHAM CHRISTIE'S LIFE
prior to 1927

This chapter draws on the information and family cuttings from Mrs Bonham Christie's great grandson, Robert.

Mrs Bonham Christie was born Mary Florence Whitburn on July 5 1865, the daughter of Mr and Mrs Charles Joseph Sofer Whitburn. When Charles Whitburn died in 1912 (born 1836) he left £1½ million. However during his younger life and early married life he was comparatively poor. On the sudden death of his father in 1850 he had to leave his private school as the fees could not be met, and he started work. He was employed by Sanderson and Company, billbrokers, but in 1859 they went bankrupt. Aged 23 he and a Mr Reeves started a discounting/banking business, which prospered 'through caution and hard work'. He was 76 years old and still working when he died in 1912. His obituary included 'He commenced life as a poor man and ended as a rich one. Like our merchant princes in commerce he achieved something more than wealth, for it is men of his calibre who have contributed to the greatness of our reputation in the world of commerce and finance'.

Charles Whitburn never had a private office. He continued working at his original desk in the Lombard Street office 'to be more in touch and more in the centre of the business'. He instructed his butler to hand him only two cigars each day; one to smoke on his train journey to work and one for his return journey. Even when his daughter Mary was a young lady her mother would double darn her new woollen stockings to ensure they lasted longer (as she mentioned in a conversation with Barry Guest 1960). His partner Reeves retired in 1878. Mary's brother Charles joined the business in 1892.

Charles Whitburn senior had a country residence at Addington Park in Kent. It is said that he had a small circle of real friends outside business rather than a large number of acquaintances. This also could be said of his daughter when she owned Brownsea Island. He had a passion for the care of dumb animals – particularly dogs. His obituary noted: 'He had one hobby – he did everything to prevent the destruction of life. He was the salvation of many a stray and derelict animal. Many old animal friends were pensioned off rather than destroyed. He once picked up a stray dog in the City, put it in his car and took it home to Ennismore Gardens, his London home, and then to Addington Park. Now there are two old mongrel dogs at Addington Park saved from the London streets'. This is thought to be where his daughter Mary developed her love and protection of animals and wild life.

It was said that Mary Whitburn was not the prettiest of girls but that she showed a great deal of character and determination from an early age. Her great grandson presumes that she was educated at home by a governess, the normal way for a daughter in a well-to-do Victorian family. She was an accomplished horsewoman and it is said that she was deeply upset when her horse died.

In 1960 Mrs Bonham Christie told Barry Guest of another example of her frugal upbringing. She had a serious accident and she could not see to read for a while. The doctor recommended a specialist who not only charged a fee of five guineas but, to her father's dismay, advised a second opinion which would cost another five guineas.

Addington Park, West Malling near Tunbridge Wells was an extremely large house – 200 feet from end to end and at least 60 feet deep. Coincidentally, this estate and others she later lived in, Marston near Frome, and Brownsea Island, were on the edge of oilfields. Like her friends, she was presented at Court in 1882 and 'did the season' from her father's London house in Ennismore Gardens.

Mary Whitburn married Captain Robert Bonham Bax Christie of the 3rd Battalion Royal Scots Fusiliers of Turville Court, Henley in March 1895 and initially lived at Birling House, a large house at West Malling. Captain Christie was the second son of Robert Christie of Fulwood Park, Liverpool – the second generation to live there. The family traded in cotton. Fulwood Park was on the banks of the Mersey about 3 miles from the centre of Liverpool. From the entrance to the house was a quarter of a mile drive. The house was in a 100 acre deer park – it was built on before the Second World War. the village on the other side of the road from Fulwood Park was Toxteth, another district of Liverpool.

Captain (later Major) Robert Christie was a soldier, horseman and sportsman. Shortly after his marriage he was delivering horses to South Africa and was wounded. Tiger and big game shooting were his pastimes, so that by 1905 when Mary and Robert Christie purchased, for about £50,000, the Marston estate near Frome, he had sufficient trophies to decorate the 50 feet square entrance hall and grand staircase at Marston House. The Marston estate was a modern agricultural and sporting estate. Major Christie extended the estate by buying land from Lord Bath and the Duke of Somerset. He modernised the house by installing central heating and generating electricity from their own gas plant (thought to be similar to the generation of electricity on Brownsea Island). The estate had 6 farms, a 25 acre lake and 200 acres of woodland.

Robert and Mary Christie had two children, a son Robert Arthur, and a daughter Elsie. They were both married before the First World War, Robert Arthur to Thela Leech and Elsie to Clement Woodbine Parish. Thela and Robert Arthur Christie had a son John but Thela died in a flu epidemic. Later Robert Arthur married Dorothea McKenzie (Mackenzie) the wealthy daughter of Nicholas Charrington a brewer.

After the First World War, Robert Christie was still hunting, particularly in Africa, spending much of his time away from Marston, whilst Mary Christie was

Animal Trophies and Skins at Marston House entrance hall.

taking more interest in the preservation of animals. There was a major family row over the handling of the family trusts by Mary's brother. Eventually the Reeves Whitburn bank was taken over and Mary and Robert Christie separated. One wonders whether or not the disputes were just about finance. Hunting trophies were displayed in the entrance hall and staircase of Marston House. There were 'dozens of heads' and 'scores of skins' of lions, tigers, rhinoceros, zebra, antelope, stags and giant bears.

The management of the Marston estate deteriorated. The gamekeeper at Marston took early retirement, was not replaced, and his cottage was left empty. Rabbits took over the lawns. Some of the donkeys saved from London costermongers became lame but were not put down. The household and estate staff was reduced.

Sometime in the early 1920s Mrs Christie left Marston and bought The Gables in Sea Road, Southbourne. It was known by the press as the 'house with the curtains drawn across', even on the sunniest of days. She built a large garage 'as big as a good sized house', to house her three cars. When new buildings began to spring up she bought a large tract of land nearby and fenced it off.

Mrs Bonham Christie, although she did not chat to many of the local residents, did converse with Mrs Dingley who had the dairy shop in St Catherine's Terrace. Her daughter (Iris Gray) believes they must have been quite friendly because Mrs Dingley visited Mrs Bonham Christie in Strathallan Nursing Home when she had an arm or leg injury in 1949 or 1950. Soon afterwards Mrs Dingley and her daughter were invited to the Castle for tea.

In 1927, Mary Christie bought Brownsea Island. It was described by her husband in a letter as ' Mary's second white elephant' – Marston being the first.

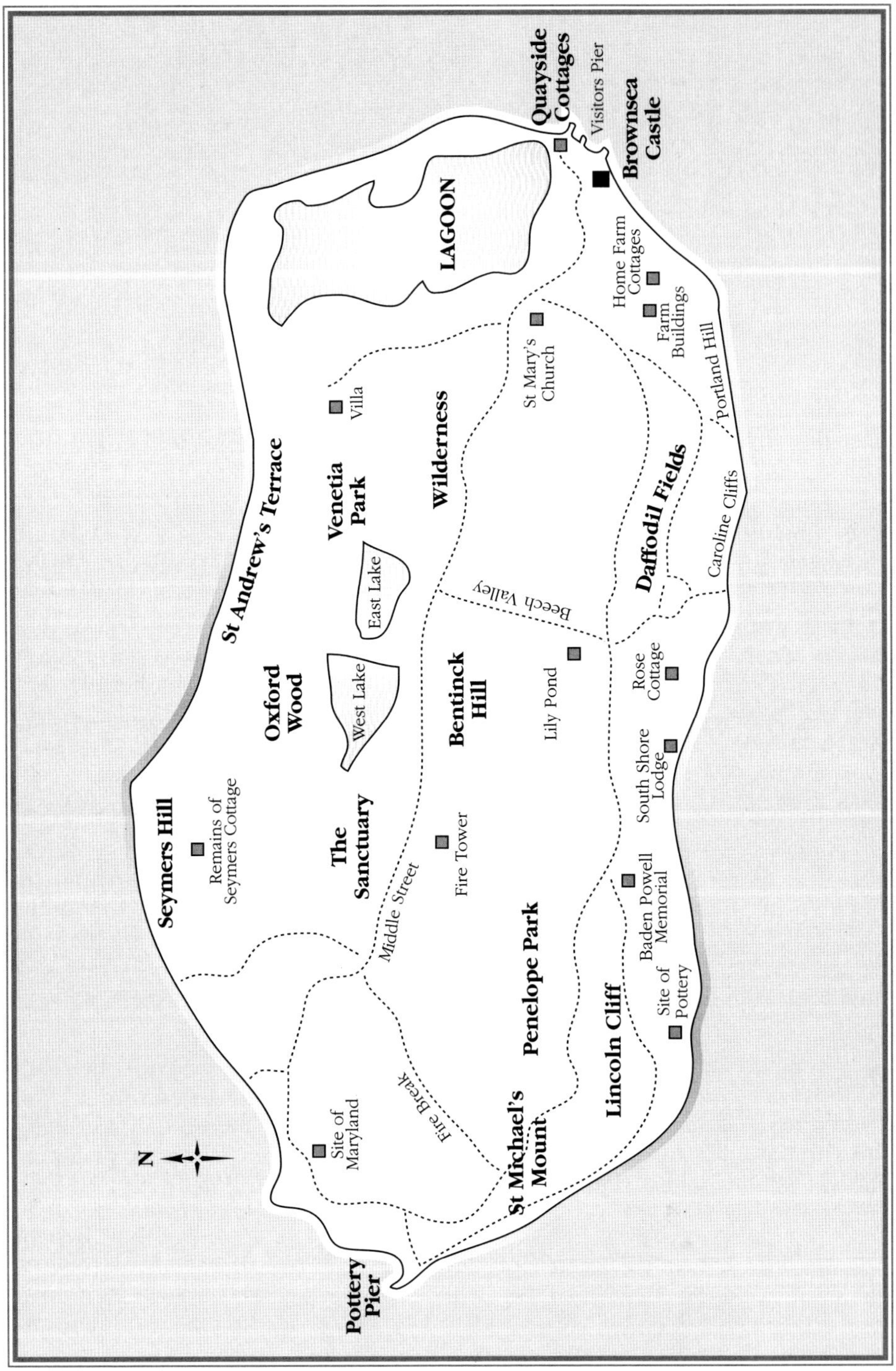

Sketch of Brownsea Island, east to West 1½ miles. (There is restricted access to parts of the Island)

BROWNSEA ISLAND

before 1927

Brownsea is an island of about 560 acres in Poole Harbour. An island area is measured usually to the high water mark and in the 1899 advertisement for the sale of the Island, the area is given as 750 acres. This is calculated to the low water mark. This has caused controversy when building/coastal protection work has been carried out (for instance in Mrs Bonham Christie's ownership) and with local people digging for cockles and baitworm during Mrs Bonham Christie's and early National Trust ownership.

In the 10th century and later, the monks from the Abbey of Cerne came to the Island, built a tiny chapel (dedicated to St Andrew) and a hermit monk was the resident. During renovations to the farm cottages in 1974 and 1979, seven skeletons from Christian graves (from the position of the skeletons), were found. These dated between 1100 and 1400 AD. Some graves may have been those of monks who died on the Island but perhaps also the graves of sailors from passing boats.

In 1540, Henry VIII initiated the building of a substantial blockhouse, with walls 44 feet long, 9½ feet wide, a moat on 3 sides, a 23 ft. drawbridge and barbican walls 4½ ft. thick. The Island is well placed to protect or control the entrance to Poole Harbour and Henry VIII used it as part of the chain of defences around South and South East England against the French and later against the Spanish. The present Castle was developed from the blockhouse to become the main residence on the Island and little remains to be seen of the original.

Ownership of an island is an ideal situation for someone who wishes to be different – an eccentric. On an island in modern times eccentricities will be severely restricted by present day laws, human rights legislation and, so far as Brownsea Island is concerned, by the ownership of the National Trust. But it was not always so. In 1722, "Auditor" Benson, later known as "Mad" Benson, was the first private person to own the Island and perhaps the most eccentric of its owners. The tales of black magic on the Island, weird noises and the subsequent burning of all his books in a fit of depression were exaggerated and repeated by generations of fisher-folk. Some of the tales of weird noises have been erroneously retold in the press as though they occurred during Mrs Christie's ownership of the Island.

Castle East front and Formal gardens during Mr & Mrs van Raalte's ownership.

Villa. Built 1852 as a rectory - never used as a rectory

POOLE HISTORICAL TRUST
Thank you for buying this book.

You may be interested in our next publication, a fascinating autobiography, due shortly.

It is in hardback, entitled
"I Was There".
(The Autobiography of Joshua Sieger)

Joshua Sieger, CBE, was an inventor and a pioneer of developments in early wireless and colour television, and worked on radar at Worth Matravers in World War II. After the War he invented a world-beating gas detection device and founded a very successful local manufacturing firm and the Wessex Export Club.

A fascinating account of the man, his family and business life.

Approx 200pp, fully illustrated. Price TBA

If you have registered your name and address with us, you will receive an order form enabling you to purchase a copy at a discounted price pre-publication.

If your name is not already on the list, write to Poole Historical Trust at the address overleaf

POOLE HISTORICAL TRUST

Titles in Print

A PORTFOLIO OF OLD POOLE	£10.99
ALBUM OF OLD POOLE	£10.99
ART IN POOLE AND DORSET	£9.99
BROWNSEA ISLANDER	£10.99
D-DAY, POOLE (Booklet)	£3
FOR NATURE, NOT HUMANS	£9.99
LIFEBOATMEN NEVER TURN BACK	£9.99
POOLE AFTER WORLD WAR II	£9.99
POOLE AND WORLD WAR II	£11.99
POOLE WAS MY OYSTER	£9.99
POOLE'S PRIDE REGAINED	£14.99
SCHOOLS OF OLD POOLE	£9.99
SPIRIT OF POOLE	£11.99
THE PRIDE OF POOLE	£11.75
VICTORIAN POOLE	£12.90

These books may be obtained from local bookshops in the area from Wareham to Blandford and Christchurch. Internet sites also offer facilities for ordering. In case of difficulty books may be ordered by post at the above prices, plus post and packing.

Write to: Poole Historical Trust,
103 Orchard Avenue,
Parkstone
Poole, Dorset. BH14 8AH
Or e-mail pht@ikda.demon.co.uk

Poole Historical Trust, founded in 1974, is a registered charity (No 271603)

The history of the Island can be found in other publications, but a brief summary of the history of the Island over the 125 years before Mrs Christie's ownership in 1927 will help to describe the people and properties on the Island when she bought it.

In 1852, Colonel Waugh and his wife Mary brought Brownsea Island for £13,000 from Lady Albinia Foster. It was thought that the Island clay could be used to make high-class tableware and figurines and yield a profit of millions of pounds. With this figure in mind, Colonel Waugh borrowed thousands of pounds to build on the Island both a large pottery with a main building of brick, measuring 200ft by over 60ft, with drying sheds and a chimney 70 ft high, and a little pottery, 150 ft long, along the south-western side of the Island. A small village was built, called Maryland - Mrs Waugh's first name was Mary - on the west side of the Island. On the eastern side of the Island, St Mary's Church was built for £10,000 with a rectory (now the Villa used by the Dorset Wildlife Trust). A "model" farm was built using plans displayed at the 1851 Exhibition. To be more self-supporting for a population of over 250, a wall was built across the mud flats of St Andrew's Bay and the area was drained to make more pasture land. However, the clay on the Island was only suitable for making bricks, sewage pipes, tiles and terracotta ware. By the time they were transported to the mainland they were too expensive as similar products were being made nearer to where they were needed. After just over 3 years Colonel and Mrs Waugh hastily left the Island, reported to be £665,000 in debt.

Another owner of Brownsea Island was the Right Honourable George

Maryland - 1927

Frederick Cavendish Bentinck MP, from 1871 to 1891. He tried unsuccessfully to revive the pottery industry. He was a collector of things Italian and Venetian, which he brought to the Island for the Castle and Church and their grounds. He gave the cottages at the eastern end of the island Italian names – Villano is one of the few names remaining. The rectory is called the Villa and the gardens developed around it are called Venetia Park, named after his sister Venetia. The population of the Island was 270 in 1881.

In Major Kenneth Robert Balfour's ownership after 1891, the Castle was gutted by fire in 1896. The Castle was restored and a new west wing added between 1897 and 1901.

In 1901 Charles and Florence van Raalte bought the Island as their country estate. Guests, including royalty, came from all over Europe to stay at the Castle. Frequent guests included Guglielmo Marconi who was experimenting with wireless telegraphy from the Haven Hotel, and Major General Robert Baden-Powell who arranged the first experimental Scout Camp on the Island. On one day over 800 guests were entertained. A 9-hole golf course, with a

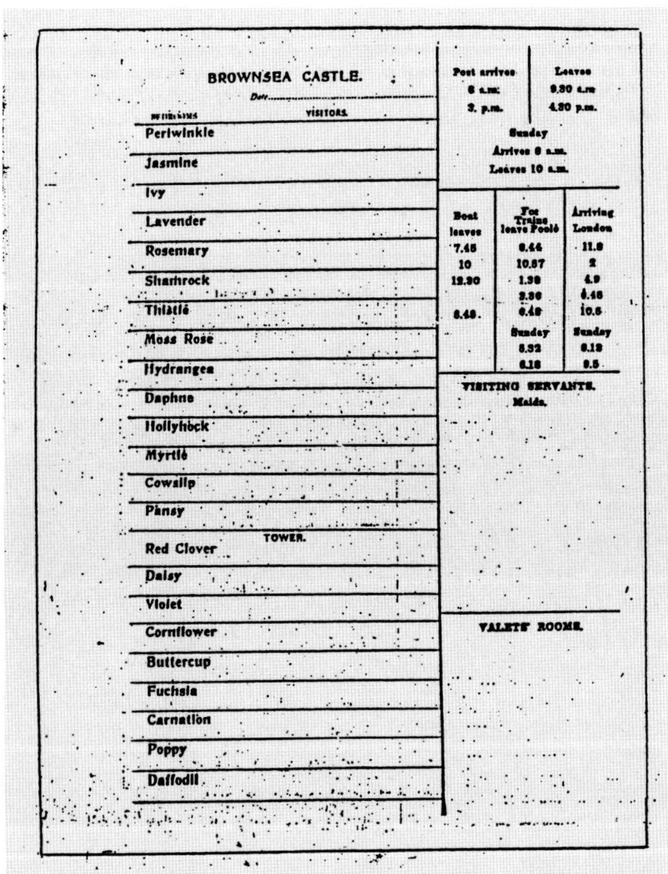
BROWNSEA CASTLE.

Date........

BEDROOMS	VISITORS
Periwinkle	
Jasmine	
Ivy	
Lavender	
Rosemary	
Shamrock	
Thistle	
Moss Rose	
Hydrangea	
Daphne	
Hollyhock	
Myrtle	
Cowslip	
Pansy	
TOWER.	
Red Clover	
Daisy	
Violet	
Cornflower	
Buttercup	
Fuchsia	
Carnation	
Poppy	
Daffodil	

Post arrives	Leaves
8 a.m.	9.30 a.m.
3. p.m.	4.30 p.m.

Sunday
Arrives 8 a.m.
Leaves 10 a.m.

Boat leaves	For Trains leave Poole	Arriving London
7.45	8.44	11.9
10	10.57	2
12.30	1.38	4.9
	3.36	6.45
6.48	6.48	10.5
	Sunday	Sunday
	5.32	9.12
	6.18	9.5

VISITING SERVANTS.
Maids.

VALETS' ROOMS.

Castle Guest information card, used by Mr & Mrs Van Raalte.

golf professional was established. Shooting parties were arranged. Over 2,000 pheasants were bred every year. More employment was available to domestic staff and estate workers. In Mr Van Raalte's time he employed:

	Employees
Steam yacht 120 tons	*9*
Steam yacht 20 tons	*3*
Launch driver	*1*
Steward	*1*
Stables at Sandbanks	*6*
Servants in the Castle	*12*
Laundry maids	*2*
Carpenters	*3*
Painters	*3*
Bricklayers	*1*
Bricklayer's labourer	*1*
On the farm	*7*
Gardeners	*10*
Gamekeepers	*4*
Estate hands	*2*
Handyman	*1*
Schoolteachers	*2*
Professional Golfer	*1*
Electricians	*2*
TOTAL	***71***

The van Raalte family had made its money from cigar manufacturing in Holland. In their household there was little of the upper class atmosphere prevalent in many country estates, and the inhabitants of the Island enjoyed working for them. The daffodil industry on the Island was started by Mrs van Raalte in 1908. Most of the new male employees had to be musicians to be able to play in the Estate Band, playing part-time at the Castle, and at mainland functions. Because fathers were musicians, their families were often very musical as well. In 1904 there were 52 children in the Island school. Boys left at 13 or 14 years. Girls left earlier if they could read, write and do simple sums! One punishment noted by Lou Brayley (nee Campbell) was to stay in and clean the schoolrooms.

Charles van Raalte died in India at the end of December 1907. Florence van Raalte continued entertaining but the First World War was a time of great change as it took away many of the men folk. After the war Florence spent more time at her London residence and her son-in-law, Lord Howard de Walden, who married Margherita van Raalte in 1912, managed the Island.

In 1925, Sir Arthur Wheeler, a wealthy stockbroker from Leicester and owner of the Haven Hotel at Sandbanks, bought the Island for £60,000. He was hoping to use the Castle as a hotel and to flood the St Andrew's Bay pastureland to make it a yacht haven. When the local authority stopped this, he sold the furnishings, tapestries, pictures and statuettes. In November 1927 the Island was sold to Mrs Mary Florence Bonham Christie.

Brownsea Island, c 1930.

Brownsea Island

1927 –1939

The Conveyance of Brownsea Island, dated 28 October 1927, was 'to Charterhouse Investment Trust Ltd and Mary Florence Christie of the Gables Southbourne in the County of Hampshire, wife of Major Robert Bonham Christie'. There is no record that her husband ever went to Brownsea Island. Some reports give the impression that he had died but this conveyance, and a letter he wrote dated April 1928, show otherwise! At that time he had 'rooms at Bognor Regis and spent a lot of time at his London club'.

Included in the purchase was a 'piece of land and buildings on the mainland at Sandbanks'. This was a house near the Coastguard Cottages and next to the Royal Motor Yacht Club known as Branksea or Branksea House. It had outbuildings used by Charles van Raalte to house his carriage and horses and later his motorcars. Also included was 'the right to use the Haven Pier free of toll'. Excluded was 'the Church and Churchyard of Saint Mary', built in the 1850s for Col. Waugh, and owned by the Church authorities. Mr William Fox of Fox & Sons, Bournemouth, negotiated the purchase of the Island. The purchase price for the Island has been variously reported as £120,000, £125,000, £127,000 and even £100,000. By contrast, two years previously Sir Arthur Wheeler had paid £60,000 for the Island estate.

The Island had been widely advertised – there is one advertisement in French – by Messrs Hankinson & Son, Land Agents and Surveyors. In the sales brochure, the Castle is described in detail as an impressive gentleman's country residence. There are full-page pictures with flowery language describing the Island estate. The Castle had 38 bedrooms – named in the van Raalte period with names of flowers so that the guests and their servants could remember their bedrooms – and many associated rooms used by the servants. The buildings on the Island estate included a farm with three cottages, cottages on the quay and near the Castle, and the village at Maryland built for the pottery workers in thee1850s. Other cottages were Seymer's Cottage and four cottages on the south side of the Island – Rose Cottage, South Lodge, St Mark's Lodge and a cottage near the Baden Powell 1907 experimental scout site. The Villa – initially built in the 1850s for a resident Vicar but never used as a vicarage – and the adjacent Venetia Park was described as 'a happy valley in which palms and other exotics luxuriate'. 'Between pines the ever changing panorama of sea and harbour can be viewed' is the walk along the South Cliffs. For Mrs

Dean home 1920's Maryland.

Bonham Christie most of the estate agents' descriptions were unimportant, as she had bought the Island as an estate with the sea replacing the usual walled perimeter as a natural reserve for birds and animals.

In 1927 an estate owner who did not allow hunting and shooting pastimes to take place on the estate was almost unique. To spend £125,000 and expect no financial return in a period of world economic depression would certainly have been remarkable. In 1925 the previous owner of the Island had said that he had bought the Island as a retreat from the business world but he soon applied for planning permission to develop the Castle and Island as a holiday business. It was soon obvious that Mrs Bonham Christie would keep her word and let nature take its course without human intervention.

In 1881 the population of the Island was 270, including children. In the van Raalte ownership the population was less than 150 (121 in the 1921 census). At Maryland many of the adjacent pairs of cottages had been combined into single dwellings to help those families who had a large number of children. At one stage there were 71 on the payroll (see Chapter 2) although about 6 were living on the mainland.

Gwen Toms noted that 'She told Dad (Fred Toms) that she did not need any of the islanders to stay – meaning she wanted them to leave'. The Toms family left the Island in 1928. Cecil Martin had worked on the Island from 1920. Daughter Ella, born in 1920, went to school on the Island. Twins Peter and Leonard Martin were born and christened on the Island in 1927. They lived in a cottage on the quay, next door to the Battricks. Leonard remembers his parents telling him that families were only allowed off the Island every fortnight and that Mrs Christie saw his mother pushing the twins in a pram on the quay and remarked that they were beautiful babies. Two weeks later, his father had notice to quit. Mr Martin was so incensed that he said that if he had had a gun he would have shot Mrs Christie. Eventually they left in 1929 and went to Longham. The only work available with accommodation was a one-bedroom cottage. The four children had to sleep on the landing at the top of the stairs. The removals from the Island can be even more traumatic than on the mainland. The islanders had to make their own arrangements and the furniture was usually piled into the cattle/coal barge. The Dean family had been working and living on the Island for four generations (1840 to 1927), but left '15 months after Mrs Christie bought the Island'. Steward 'Tresco' Brown (there were two families with the name Brown in the 20th century on the Island), brought to the Island to develop the daffodil industry in 1908, left soon after Mrs Christie arrived.

The families living at Maryland had even more problems when they left the Island. Although the cattle barge could be loaded with furniture directly from the quay at the eastern end of the Island, at Maryland the barge had to be anchored off shore and the furniture had to be manhandled out to the barge wading through the waters. Although the exodus from the Island started in 1927 there were still people living at Maryland in 1934 – maybe just one family, Mrs Phillips and her two disabled daughters. They left around the time of the fire on the Island in July 1934 with the help of St John's Ambulance.

In 1928 Dorothy Battrick, aged 9, was the only pupil at the Island school and the authorities closed it. At the church the last christening (before 1964) was 7 August 1932, the last marriage (before 1963) was in 1924, the last burial (before 1969) was 28 August 1927. Miss Dibben remembers being invited to a church service by Mr Campbell. Other than herself there were the Hutchings and the Campbells. The church closed when Mr Campbell left the Island in 1936.

Improvements and renovations were undertaken at the Castle but Mrs Bonham Christie continued to live in the Agent's house – the end house on the quay, now used by the National Trust Property Manager. Mrs Lou Brayley said that her father, Mr Alfred Campbell was Steward (i.e. Island Estate Manager) from 1928 until he left the Island in 1936. Because Mrs Bonham Christie was living at the Agent's house they lived in the 'long house' next to the coal store (now the National Trust's visitor reception area). The workshop was above the coal store. Also living in the Quay Cottages were the Battricks (they left the Island early in 1929 and their story is told in Poole Historical Trust's "Brownsea Islander") and the boatman. In Chapter 4 it will be noted that Mrs Bonham Christie lived in the Castle during World War II, although when the refugees came from the Netherlands to the Island in 1940 she was still living in the Agent's house on the quay.

Mrs Eva Norman, whose father had been Head Gamekeeper to Major Balfour for three years and had returned in 1904 to work for Mr van Raalte, remembers visiting the Campbells in 1934, she thought. She says that Mr Campbell and daughter Lou were looking after Mrs Christie. Mrs Christie lived in the Agent's house. She does not remember seeing any red squirrels – at the time they were common on the mainland so may not have been noticed. Deer, 'plenty' of rats and wild fowl were seen. There were 'mosquitoes by the million.'

Someone considered eccentric made good copy for a story in the local and national press. The Sunday Express, 20 August 1932 is an example. The reporter managed to persuade a boatman to take him to the Island. The boatman told him to find the foreman (Mr Campbell then) to get permission to approach Mrs Christie. The reporter saw 'piles of loose hay to feed the rabbits, calves as big as cows, an expensive sea wall built for the ducks but instead rats – great big fellows – played on it'. Eventually he found the foreman who told him that 'The Lady of the Lonely Isle' would see no one. There were eight people on the Island. The foreman's daughter (Louise

Mrs Bonham Christie and grandson, John, in the 1930's.

Campbell) looks after Mrs Christie and leaves the Island only once a week to buy stores. On Sunday she (this refers to Lou Campbell but in the report and others based on the same information the 'she' is taken as Mrs Christie) plays the organ in the Gothic Church. The article continues 'She lives in a small cottage not the Castle and rises at 2.15 every afternoon. She goes to bed as dawn breaks over the Island. Candle in hand she potters about in the night. She is unafraid of the animals that sport at her feet etc. She is clothed all in black'

In another newspaper – possibly with information from the same reporter under the headlines 'Sick Queen of Lone Isle. Rich Castle owner ill in Cottage'. This article goes further stating this time that there were fewer than 20 people living on the Island (in 1932, fewer than 20 adults is possibly correct). The school is closed, the cottage roofs have fallen in and a massive sea wall has been built in order that wild ducks may rest undisturbed. An employee has said that she was ill with rheumatic fever and had not been seen for five months. As well as reporting that she had refused to see a doctor it added that one had visited the Island twice! The reporter continues 'One fisherman told of weird cries heard in the night and shadowy forms seen through the trees possibly due to Mrs Christie refusing to have any animals destroyed'. She was said to have used only the business room in the Castle since she arrived.

When other stories relating to Mrs Christie or to Brownsea Island were printed the previously published background information was often used. On 22 December 1932 an unknown national newspaper had headlines 'Mysterious Fire at Queen of Brownsea Closed House'. This refers to the Gables, Southbourne, not used but still owned by Mrs Christie. It was mentioned that she was 86 years old (possibly a misprint for 66). This was too much for Mrs Christie and extracts from her letter with comments were published. In defence the newspaper states that the information was telegraphed from a leading news agency but then adds to the confusion by calling Mrs Bonham Christie 'Mrs Marston-Biggot'. Marston Bigot was her estate, still owned, near Frome! Mrs Christie writes, 'I do not live a lonely life. There are many more than 8 living on the Island. I am certainly not known in Dorset as The Lady of the Lonely Isle. I am nothing like as old as you state (86). I never expect to even live to that age. The whole Island is not reserved for nature. Hay is not placed in the fields for rabbits. In fact I do not believe rabbits eat hay. I do not play the organ in the church and I am not living in a cottage. I am living temporary in the Agent's house while new drainage, new water system etc. are being installed and other repairs and renewals are done to the Castle. Certain animals have to be killed and kept down in numbers so your remarks that no living thing is harmed are incorrect. There is no sea wall on the Island to protect the wild ducks'. The newspaper concludes, 'We gladly publish her letter and offer her our sincere regrets that any mis-statement we unwittingly published should have caused her inconvenience or annoyance'.

In spite of her denials, Mrs Christie – a keen supporter of the RSPCA – even before she had completed the purchase of the Island, had questioned one of the tenants on the Island about a canary in a cage. When told that the canary was rarely let out of the cage she said that she would not allow any birds to be caged or any birds or animals to be killed. When she took possession of the Island, this policy was extended: no killing of animals, no blood sports, and farm animals were to roam freely. Horses were not to be harnessed and cows not be to milked. The horses would not be needed to plough land. Transporting coal from the eastern deep-water quay to Maryland village on the western side of the Island, and moving furniture in the other direction (when evicted from Maryland) could not be by horse and cart. In the late 1940s and early 1950s (see Chapter 5) there was one horse and two cows still alive on the Island. One cow was aged 36 years when it died. They grazed freely and an employed Island keeper gave them hay. There is no record of this supplementary feeding in the 1930s but there are various reports of mainland residents including evicted islanders feeding the farm animals on the beaches.

There is a letter dated 26 November 1928 from the office of Commissions of Crown Lands stating 'The Crown does not claim the Foreshore between high and low water mark of Brownsea, or Branksea Island......... therefore this area of foreshore belongs to the owner'. 'Private Property Landing Prohibited' and 'Private Property' notices were on the beaches during the van Raalte period. No one was allowed to land without permission. When Mrs Christie went on the Island before the purchase was completed, she had to have a permit to land. Before Mrs Christie arrived, there were trips to the mainland and visitors including family visitors to the Island. With so many employed on the Island any unwanted visitors, poachers etc would have been seen on or soon after landing. Mrs Christie enforced the 'no landing without permission' rule. To the mainland teenagers with boats, this was seen as an added 'adventure' (see Chapter 5). In 1933, Fred Effamy, about 14 years old, often went to Brownsea Island by boat with three other boys. They knew there was likely to be someone on patrol so they seldom left the beach. One evening it was getting dark and a 'gamekeeper' (Mrs Christie would possibly call him a keeper!) caught hold of him. The other three ran off and launched their boat. Fred was taken to Mrs Christie and his wife told me that he was detained overnight. 'Detained' may be too strong a term but as his boat had left the Island he could not return to the mainland. Fred's mother went to the police and he was 'released' from the Island the next day.

Not so lucky was Miss Audrey Batt and her father, a local tailor. Mr Batt, a keen fisherman, had for 30 years been digging for worms for bait on Brownsea Island foreshore. He ignored a warning letter sent in 1930 by Mrs

Harry Reeves, Water Postman – note the "no live bait" notice

Christie's solicitors that he had committed a trespass. As well as owning the foreshore, killing worms or fishing were abhorrent to her. A fracas occurred on 19 August 1933 when one of Mrs Christie's employees set his boat loose whilst Mr Batt was on the shore. Later Mrs Christie returned his boat with the warning that 'If you come here again, my servants have orders to throw you and anybody with you into the sea'.

The Daily Mail on 11 October 1933 had front page headlines about a Swanage Magistrates' Court case. Other national and local papers reported the proceedings as well. On the 2 September 1933, Mr Batt was digging on the foreshore while his daughter was near the boat, which was anchored in shallow water. Suddenly an outboard motor boat with a Miss Olsen and 16-year-old Etonian, John Christie, Mrs Christie's grandson, appeared. Miss Batt jumped into her father's boat, Miss Olsen pulled up the anchor of this boat and John Christie towed it into deep water. Miss Olsen jumped into the boat with Miss Batt, and after checking she could swim, picked her up 'like a sack of wool' and threw her into the sea. Miss Olsen then grabbed hold of Mr Batt by his trousers and although they were made of stiff canvas they tore as she tried to throw him into the sea after his daughter. Miss Bertha Olsen, aged 26, a native of Denmark, was a physical fitness expert. The family story was that she was a companion to Mrs Christie and a governess for her grandchildren when they were on the Island. In court the prosecutor maintained that Miss Olsen was employed to deal with intruders. It was reported that Mrs Christie appeared in court dressed entirely in black and wore a wide brimmed hat with a large black plume. The charge against her for procuring the assault was dismissed. Miss Olsen, reported as the 'Amazon', who left the country soon after the case, was fined 40 shillings (£2) and John Christie, 20 shillings.

For several years Mrs Christie had a dispute with Poole Harbour Board over her strengthening the sea wall in the 1930s. The Harbour Board had written to Mrs Christie's solicitor requesting plans for the work she had authorised on the sea wall below the high water mark. Mrs Christie must have seen the news report of a Harbour Board meeting - her solicitor was on holiday, so she replied directly. She wrote that her solicitor had shown her two letters. It was only repair work and was within the boundary of her property. It was therefore no concern of the Board and they had no right to demand any plans. Her final response was to tell the Harbour Board that she could not show them the plans at any rate, as she had no plans!

The report of the next Harbour Board meeting stated that the new work on the sea wall projected about two feet beyond the old works for a considerable length of the Island. The Board did not necessarily object to the work but certainly taking shingle from the shore could only be allowed by permission from the Board. The Harbour Act of 1914 was quoted.It was noted that the work had been going on for over two years and they would write to Mrs Christie explaining the procedures!

Poachers were another problem. In August 1933 there was a report of a Wareham Police (possibly Magistrates) Court. They considered a case for a full day on evidence 'laid on behalf of the owner of Brownsea Island, Mrs Bonham Christie' of trespass against five alleged poachers, one of whom lived locally at Bridge House, Longham. It later transpired that the owner of Bridge House organised wild fowl shooting for his paying guests. It was alleged that the defendants were seen to shoot over a wall at St Andrew's Bay – then marsh land and now the lagoon. On the 14 January (year unknown – probably 1934) three workers on the sea wall gave evidence that firing over St Andrew's Bay had taken place and one of the defendants was on the wall and another crawling along it. Alfred Campbell the foreman employed by Mrs Christie gave evidence that at low tide the water went to within 100-200 yards of the wall and at high tide came up to the wall but varied from place to place along the wall. There were notices 'Private Property to Low-Water mark'. At 4 pm Mr Campbell was in his cottage and heard 'tremendous gunfire from sporting guns'. He went round the wall and just beyond the workmen's landing stage saw a motor boat close in shore. The defendants got into their boat and pushed off. Mr Campbell found a shot curlew ten yards inside the wall and several cartridges. Questioned by the defence solictor Mr Campbell agreed that notice boards taken down two years previously when work started on the wall had not been replaced. It was stated that the shooting was for wild fowl and this was done below the low-water mark where Mrs Christie had no authority. They wore waders. At the end of a day of legal arguments the magistrates dismissed the case against the five defendants, as there had not been sufficient evidence that they were trespassing in search of game.

Mrs Christie continued to try to stop intruders interfering with her nature reserve but on the 18 July 1934 the ultimate fear was realised. A fire was out of control on the Island. Front-page headlines were in national and local papers. Flames could be seen 50 feet high from two miles away. Many mainland residents remember the awesome sight from their childhood some 67 years ago. Crowds gathered at Constitution Hill and on the mainland shores. One newspaper even claimed that the smoke could be seen from the coast of France.

Initially 68-year-old Mrs Bonham Christie (reported in the Daily Mirror as an 88-year-old) led her twelve staff trying to save the Island. There was a delay in getting fire pumps from the mainland to the Island because of the difficulty of loading them onto boats or barges but it was also said that Mrs Christie was trying to negotiate a lower price to transport them to the Island. When pumps did manage to reach the Island a fresh south-westerly wind had spread the fire over half the Island. Fire hydrants installed after the Castle was gutted by fire in 1896 had been neglected and were useless. Eventually seawater was used. As well as firemen, local fishermen and boatmen forgot their disputes and went to the Island to cut firebreaks. Gerry Luff's daughters told me that their father – Harvey's boatman – did not come home for five days. He was ferrying people and supplies to and from the Island as well as assisting on the Island. One day his future wife did not recognise the bearded and smoke blackened

Island Fire, July 1934.

person in Poole High Street. Often he told his daughters of his memories of those hectic and frightening days. As well as the flames and choking smoke he remembers clearly seeing, in the moonlight, the antlers of the deer just above the water as they were swimming across the harbour. Dark patches on the water were scores of rats swimming away from the Island.

Whilst the fire was raging, altar hangings and ornaments were removed from the Church for safety. In a photograph in the Bournemouth Evening Echo dated 19 July 1934 furniture and belongings from Maryland are piled on the beach. The last occupants from Maryland were leaving at this time and their belongings may have been carried to the beach ready to wade out to the cattle/coal barge offshore before the fire started.

Most of the fire damage was on two thirds of the Island to the west of a line through what is now called Beech Valley. Some cottages had been fire damaged including Maryland village. Luckily, the Church, farm buildings, Castle and cottages near the quay only had smoke damage but the vegetation, animals and birds had suffered. At the height of the blaze squeals of animals could be heard as they charged through the undergrowth to escape the fire. Many, together with the birds, must have perished. Two deer with burnt hooves cowering in a shed had to be put down. At first it was thought that Sea Scouts camping officially on the Island had started the fire, but one of the evicted villagers from Maryland later confessed to Jack Battrick that he had started it as an act of revenge. According to fishermen a tinker who had been prosecuted for stealing daffodils from the island had started the fire. When wisps of smoke were first seen the tinker in his "Poole" canoe was near the island.

In 1932 a fire at The Gables, Southbourne was reported in the Evening Standard, Evening Post, and others with headlines 'Mysterious Fire at the Queen of Brownsea's Closed House'. It had been left unoccupied since Mrs Christie had moved to Brownsea Island. The report added that there were several cars in the locked-up garage which had never been used. The report states that £600 worth of damage was done. It had been noticed that tramps had sheltered in the house. An open window supported the theory that the tramps had caused the fire. In May 1935 it was reported in the Daily Mail and local papers that Mrs Christie had refused to sell to Bournemouth Corporation the large plot of land on the cliffs at Southbourne which she had purchased and fenced off when she was living at The Gables. Mrs Christie had said that 'If the area was public open space it would be more tempting than ever for day excursionists. Nobody wants to live near a space open to the public with their present day bad manners and their untidy ways of throwing bottles and paper about'

In November 1938 an advertisement for a worker on Brownsea Island is highlighted in the Evening News and other newspapers. The usual embellishments included 'Lonely Island Queen who does not allow any killing of animals'. In the Citizen (17 November 1938) it states that Mrs Robert Bonham Christie requires 'Bird sanctuary keeper, knowledgeable about birds, married, no school available, house found'. This article also includes the information that 'Mrs Bonham Christie would like to travel all over the world

1915 Selden two ton truck.

opening every cage of wild and tame animals'. It continues that she banned hunting over some land she owned in England. 'No one should torture and cause such suffering to any of God's creatures as the fox suffers when being hunted.'

Although Sir Arthur Wheeler had sold most of the removable sculptures and large paintings before Mrs Christie bought Brownsea Island, some furniture and fittings from the van Raalte period were left in the Castle. Horse harnesses were still hanging – and were seen still in position in the late 1940s and 1950s in the stables (demolished in 1962 as unsafe) between the farm cottages and the cowshed. There was a 1915 Selden two-ton truck, described as a 'sit up and beg model' with solid tyres in a barn. Also a Bullnose Morris brought to the Island by the van Raaltes was in a barn. A lot of furniture and belongings brought over for Mrs Christie remained stored in the Castle, some still in packing cases when she died.

The cars at Marston, it is believed, were brought down to The Gables and eventually taken to the barn/storage area at the house at Branksea on the mainland at Sandbanks. The Rolls Royce, only a chassis (no. 77AG) and engine and had 145 miles on the clock. It had been purchased in 1925 but Mrs Bonham Christie's chauffeur at Marston House gave notice soon after that and left her employment. She swore that she would never go in a car again. It is reported that she never did but this may not be completely correct. It was reported that the other cars brought down were a 1912 Mercedes Landaulette and a 1913 Fiat.

Most people considered Mrs Christie to have been a recluse whilst she owned Brownsea Island. After the Second World War this may be correct. It would seem from my enquiries that in the 1930s she, like her father, was a private person. Obviously she devoted most of her time to preserving the animal and bird life on the Island. She did have a few visitors most of whom she received in the Castle although she was living in the Agent's house on the quay. Charles Cooper, from the Estate Agents Cooper and Tanner who, with Mrs Christie's son, was managing the Marston estate would come to Brownsea Island to advise her. His wife had died young (in 1917) and from 1927 Mrs Christie invited two of the daughters (Una and Stella) to stay on the Island. A governess sometimes came with them and they stayed at the Villa (now in the Dorset Wildlife Trust Reserve). They had told their daughters that they had tea in the Castle.

The daffodils planted in Mrs van Raalte's ownership continued to bloom. This appears to be the only source of income from the Island in the 1930s and 1950s. Mr Dibben, a local fish wholesaler, had a contract and brought the pickers across to the Island. He used to put up a tent to protect the picked blooms and the pickers. In the 1930s Gerry Luff was a boatman for Harveys and would take the pickers across and boxes of daffodils to the mainland. Mrs Christie got to know Mr Luff following his assistance in the 1934 fire and she may have used his boat on her infrequent visits to the mainland. She would send him a money gift (ten shillings in 1936) and a handwritten note at Christmas. I have also seen such letters for 1935, 1936, 1937.

The 1937 letter reads:

Brownsea Island
Sandbanks
Bournemouth
22 December 1937

Dear Mr Jerry
I always forget your surname. I cannot think why and whoever I ask says the same thing so you must forgive me.
I write to wish you a Very Merry and Happy Christmas with lots of luck and fun, and am enclosing a small present of money for you to buy something which you are wanting, as I find it better to send money then people can buy what they like, and I may choose something you have already got or do not want.
We had terrible weather you must find it cold on the water during these gales and cutting winds. I hope you keep well in spite of the weather.

Yours truly

Mary Bonham Christie.

500 scouts had camped on the Island in 1927 before Mrs Christie had bought the Island. 500 scouts camped in 1932, the 25th anniversary of the experimental camp on the Island in 1907. Sea Scouts were said to be camped on the Island at the time of the 1934 fire. It is thought that no more scouts were allowed on the Island in Mrs Christie's ownership after the fire.

Gwen Jennings (née Toms) wrote to Mrs Christie in 1939 to ask if she and husband Alf could visit the Island for sentimental reasons. Her reply could not have been nicer. Mrs Jennings must have informed Mrs Christie of her father's (Fred Toms) death before she could use the permit received with the letter dated 20 July 1939. Mrs Christie's letter of condolence included another permit to land. The boatman at Sandbanks was amazed that they had permission to land. Gwen's account adds more information. She says that Mrs Christie arranged for a farm hand (implying the farm was still in operation) although it may have been a keeper, to have the church bells rung as they entered the church. It is believed that a visit to the inside of the church had not been agreed for anyone else since 1936 when the church was closed. Mrs Christie even suggested that Gwen should play the organ. They went back to her house on the quay (Mrs Christie was still living in the Agent's house and not the Castle) and she explained why people had to leave the Island when she bought it. She was surprised that they had not brought over their daughter Dulcia. As she was not named on the permit she had been left on the mainland with a friend! Mrs Christie suggested they returned with her the next week, and gave them another permit. Mrs Christie was delighted to see the three of them and said they could go anywhere on the Island and pick blackberries. When they left the Island, she gave Dulcia a kiss and said that her Grandfather Toms had been a wonderful man. They visited the Island again before they left for Australia. The ferryman - was it Gerry Luff? - who took them over from Sandbanks thought that they were the first of the previous residents to have permission to land since everyone had left.

THE WAR YEARS

1939 to 1945

Commander Dartnel, RNVR, in the 49-line poem 'The Rise and Fall of the Poole Navy' (in his booklet 'The Royal Navy at Poole 1940-45') wrote -

'On Brownsea was built a secret device for fooling the enemy raiders
But Mrs Christie, the owner, said the mat(e)lots were the real invaders'.

This sums up Mrs Christie – 80 years-old by the end of the war – still trying, against all odds at times, to keep Brownsea Island for Nature not Humans. She refused to leave the Island even when decoy fires were lit to attract German bombers to the Island. Initially she continued to live in the Agent's house on the quay, but after a year or two, moved to live in the Castle. Her Castle with its gardens she 'defended' against 'friendly' invaders. This gave another dimension to tales and rumours circulating locally. One rumour was that she was harbouring a German spy. She must have heard about this because some 20 years later she told Barry Guest of this. She said that she had known only one German – a butler some years before the war – and she remembered him as a good worker. Another rumour was that she concealed a radio transmitter in one of the Castle chimneys. Yet another, this time circulating amongst the troops was that she lit fires to guide the enemy and would not let the Fire Brigade extinguish them. This may refer to the decoy fires lit by the Royal Navy in 1942 or even the 1934 fire when the Fire Brigade was delayed – neither started by Mrs Christie!

Early in the war, mines made from torpedo warheads set in concrete were placed near the entrance to Poole Harbour. They could be electrically detonated from an observation post near the Castle. The Royal Navy staff operating this were billeted in Rose Cottage, now used by the Brownsea Island Voluntary Wardens.

Brownsea Island facing the entrance to Poole Harbour – the chain ferry now crosses the entrance – was an obvious place to install defensive armament. However the biggest 'invasion' came from refugees, first from Holland and then Belgium. When the Germans invaded Holland and Belgium in May 1940, some of the Dutch and Belgian families took to boats and set off for England. I am indebted to Barry Guest for recording an interview with Mrs Clara Douie and a policeman who were sent to the Island when the refugees arrived. The authorities in this country were concerned that amongst the refugees would be German spies or sympathisers and so all the boats were escorted to Brownsea Island. The plan was to interrogate the refugees on the Island. When satisfied, they would be sent with their boats to Weymouth and then dispersed on the mainland. Initially it was thought that the checks and interrogations would take three days for each batch of refugees. However the numbers arriving – 600 or 700 in the first week – were too large to deal with quickly. All told, nearly 3,000 refugees arrived and it took six weeks before most got to the mainland. Some were detained under Regulation 18B (aliens

Watercolour by P. Sharpe of Dutch and Belgian refugee craft off Brownsea Island.

who might be sympathisers with the enemy) and taken to Wandsworth Prison, London. It was said that there were nearly 100 vessels belonging to the refugees moored in Brownsea Roads.

When the refugees came to the Island, Mrs Christie was still living in the Agent's house on the quay. Others named at that time were boatmen Bill Baker, 'old' Bill Heath, a gardener, and his wife, and Mary and John Hilton who lived at the farm. Initially 25 policemen and a Sergeant were sent over and billeted in the School House. This number was soon reduced to four. Two policemen and a soldier patrolled the Island to ensure that the frustrated refugees did not try to move on before it was allowed. Their possessions including 'bicycles and post boxes' were taken off the boats and stored near the quay.

Marquees, soup kitchens, troughs for washing, and lavatories were hastily brought over from Poole and erected on the Island. Derek Loader remembers from the 1950s a tank with 'bullet holes in the base of it' supported on brick pillars with a brick corridor leading to it on the Church Field – at the junction of the paths near the Church wall. He thought that it was a makeshift shower used by the army but he could not understand why it was sited so far from the houses. I think that it was part of the washing arrangements set up for the refugees. Washing facilities – for personal and clothes washing – were in 'great troughs'. Some refugees had come over in boats that had carried iron ore and they were covered in grime.

Some were diamond merchants. Their coats were covered in grime but diamonds were secreted in the linings. The naval interrogators sent the diamonds to Poole police station for safekeeping. One boat owner waiting for his family in Holland was ordered at gunpoint to take a group of refugees – before his family reached the boat. Understandably he was heartbroken.

For a while the Island's water supply ran out. It was said that Mary and John Hilton had half a dozen cows, which produced some milk. Since Mrs Christie had let the cattle run free on the Island, I cannot understand that in 1940, thirteen years after their freedom, they were still producing calves and being milked. Generally it was 'wonderful weather' but the refugees were only allocated one blanket each. The ground was hard and the space in the marquees was very cramped. Mrs Christie helped with the preparation of the food and making the refugees as comfortable as possible. Mrs Christie was seen feeding gigantic rats outside her cottage on the Quay. She must have fed them well as none were seen amongst the marquees on the Church Field. The refugees were not allowed in the uninhabited cottages as they could be 'policed' more effectively when confined to the Church Field. Mothers and children slept in one marquee and the males used a tent where the Chestnut trees are now.

Miss Mary Llewellin (later to become Poole's first woman Mayor) and her stepsisters, Mrs Douie and Mrs Carey from Upton House and Girl Guides were amongst those taken to the Island to help. The Medical Officer did not want the babies looked after in the Sick Bay but Mrs Douie was not allocated another area. She was given a primus stove and a tin of Ostermilk to prepare food for the babies. She borrowed a second primus stove from Mary Hilton. Once one batch of baby food was prepared the next was started. One refugee had collected his pregnant wife from hospital and she 'hung on' across the North Sea. The baby was born in Poole Hospital.

One refugee was a senior Dutch policeman but he had to be detained on

Guides - Miss Mary Llewellin, Rene Turk (née Dunford), Audrey Willett and Sylvia Willett cousins - at the refugee camp.

Luftwaffe aerial Reconnaissance photograph of Brownsea Island in August 1941.

the Island until the full interrogation had been completed. They had left their homes hastily, made the journey, most in small fishing boats, and were then taken in convoy to Brownsea Island with limited food – or without food on the journey. Mrs Douie remembers only bread and soup being provided. They were most unhappy when they could not go to the mainland and they feared that the Germans would be invading Great Britain. The police (Jack Williams and Chubb from Sandbanks were names mentioned) patrolled armed with revolvers so that the refugees did not try to reach their boats or even swim to the mainland. Mrs Douie and Mrs Carey were sleeping in a Girl Guide tent and for their safety it was suggested that they should move to the Castle laundry building. They declined and continued to use their tent in the Church Field. When the boats left Poole to rescue the stranded soldiers at Dunkirk the refugees were upset further as their boats were requisitioned to join the flotilla.

In the taped interview, Mrs Douie mentioned the large number of cats on the Island. To reduce the number Mary Hilton collected all the tomcats together and intended to have them destroyed. However Mrs Christie did not agree to this and told Mrs Hilton to keep the tomcats away from the others! At another time a lady told me she was sent to Brownsea Island with the Land Army aiming to cultivate the land for food production. Their first job was to destroy the rats. However, 'There was an old lady on the Island who used to feed the rats'. They could not exterminate the rats and the projected cultivation on the Island did not proceed.

Flying boats were based in Poole Harbour and the requisitioned Haven Hotel near the entrance to Poole Harbour was a military headquarters. The eastern side of Brownsea Island was ideal for observation and if necessary engaging enemy ships or planes in the approaches to the Harbour. The Island was classified as a Class 'A' Strong Point of Defence in anti-invasion plans. The

Royal Navy code for the Island was P1 and its artillery battery as 6 BATT.

John Anderson in a letter dated November 1995 – when he was 76 years old – to John Barker, gives a vivid description of life on the Island in 1940, including the period when the refugees were on the Island. John Anderson was in the Navy and was recalled from leave to Portsmouth Royal Navy Barracks. They did not know where they were going but were concerned when they learned they were being sent to 'P1 6 BATT' as it did not appear to be a sea-going posting. They were more alarmed when they were issued with rifle and bayonet, 'tin' hat, ammunition pouches, water bottles etc. and sent to Whale Island (H.M.S. Excellent) for a week's land fighting course. They went by train to Poole, marched to the quay and 'piled' on to a large motorboat to Brownsea Island. They were to crew two 6-inch naval guns (reputed to have been manufactured in Turkey in 1912) until the army took over. Initially their food was cooked in a makeshift kitchen consisting of large diameter metal pipe, corrugated iron sheets (scrubbed!), mud and clods of grass. Eventually they received a First World War field kitchen. They slept under canvas although he remembers seeing empty houses. 'The old lady who owned the Island' put up a notice prohibiting fishing from the jetty with live bait. They had a male Sick Berth Attendant but no one went to his tent for treatment. Instead they saw a lady VAD (Voluntary Aid Detachment) nurse who was in one of the houses. She had not come to the Island for the naval personnel but was assisting with the Dutch and Belgian refugees. The refugee area on the Church Field was strictly out of bounds for naval personnel.

One day they had a report that someone had seen parachutists drifting towards Brownsea Island. No parachutists were found but when a Dutch coaster (probably belonging to the refugees) was blown up it was realised that mines had been parachuted into the sea. Two Dutch coasters were sunk in the Swash Channel by magnetic mines. From another source I had heard that Ivor Holloway from Hamworthy had received a Dutch bravery medal from Queen Wilhelmina for helping to rescue Dutch seamen – possibly the same incident.

John Anderson saw in an 'old broken down shed' what looked like a Model T Ford, which had been converted into a pick-up. It was used to transport shells to the two gun sites. It had 'practically no brakes' and filled sand bags were placed at both ends of the route to ensure that it did not overshoot. I remember Hugh Green talking about the Island in 1962 some 20 years later saying that one of Mrs Christie's great grandchildren gave him and his wife a ride in the Selden (believed to be the same vehicle) and the brakes were suspect, particularly worrying when they stopped close to the water on the quay!

Harry Moyle told Barry Guest that he spoke to Dick Barker (a boatman with Harveys) and was told that the six-inch naval guns were brought from Poole Quay to Brownsea Island on a dredger. They were manhandled up the cliff face to their position in the Castle grounds. The shells each weighed 100 lbs. Mr Murray told Harry Moyle that the guns were made in 1912 for the Turkish Navy.

There were 100 to 250 personnel from Royal Artillery, RAF Regiment and Royal Navy whilst he was on the Island. Searchlights were installed in the Villano (now the National Trust Coffee Shop) garden and in the South West

Covered searchlight in front of the Villano.

corner of the Castle grounds. They were to be used to light up the harbour entrance to detect enemy naval activity and were camouflaged to look like sheds. One dark stormy night they were used to help eight Royal Canadian Air Force Sunderland seaplanes land. He thought that the electricity was generated on the Island and the water was piped from the mainland. The observation post (now filled in) was through a hatch and down a ladder into the cliff side. Arthur Parrish told John Barker 'There was a good view across the harbour'.

Ex-Lance Bombardier Charles Howell (traced by John Barker) sent a letter in the 1990s recounting his wartime experiences on Brownsea Island. He first saw the Island from the Harbour Heights Hotel. He and two others were to join the observation post team of 347 Battery. The observation post was the eyes and ears for the Battery. They monitored all shipping in and out of the harbour, and relayed orders, and received messages from other Units. He mentions several names (his letter is held on the Island in the archives). A footballer, Dai Astley who had played for Aston Villa and Derby County had special mention as his presence made the battery football team unbeatable! A 347 Battery duty roster board can be seen in the National Trust Visitor Centre in the old farm buildings.

Mr Murray knew of a RN detachment on the Island but did not meet them. Most likely they were responsible for setting off the aircraft decoy system because he went on to say they were heavily bombed in 1942 by German planes. Dozens of bombs were dropped one night and one 'huge' bomb landed 10 feet away from the trench Charles Howell was in. Luckily it did not go off. Most of the bombs that night did not explode and they assumed that they had been made by forced labour from the German occupied countries. At another decoy site at Arne some of the unexploded bombs were filled with sand. (There are other explanations for the bombs not exploding – as detailed later in this chapter). Soldiers from the Engineers and Pioneer Corps came over to remove the unexploded bombs. When made safe they were taken to the Island quay which was 'littered with them'.

When there was a 'bomb alert' those not on duty at the battery had to patrol the shore. One night, Charles Howell and a Sergeant caught an exhausted German Airman who had baled out coming up the beach. From another source Flight Lieutenant (Wing Commander when he retired in 1966) Bob Doe, a British Hurricane and Spitfire pilot in the Battle of Britain (awarded the DFC for his successes), baled out and landed on Brownsea Island. His parachute had been badly shot-up in the aerial fight 'hardly a single panel without a rip in it'. He descended too quickly. He hoped that he would land in the sea to reduce the impact on landing. He landed on the Island and still had a soft landing in a midden or cesspit below the farm. Although semi-conscious when he landed he soon realised that there was a terrible stench. Standing nearby was an 'enormous fierce looking man brandishing an iron bar'. The man spoke in a broad Irish accent 'What are yer?' On reflection Bob Doe feels that he was sufficiently conscious to reply 'British' rather than 'English'. The Irish giant pulled him out of the cesspit and carried him over his shoulder to the quay.

Charles Howell goes on to describe their living arrangements. The Guard Room is now the National Trust reception area. The Quay Cottages were the billets with the last one (Agent's House) the Sergeants' Mess. Approaching the clock tower the Medical Room and Battery Office (School House and adjacent cottage) were on the right. On the left was the Cookhouse. The Officers' Mess was in the Villano.

A short stay Shore Leave on the mainland was allowed every four days and on the eighth day a 24-hour pass was issued. This was spent in the YMCA at Bournemouth where a bath was available! They were banned from going to Poole. The reason given was that sexual diseases were prevalent. This was not thought to be correct and several did go to Poole. It was estimated that the battery detachment numbered nearly 100 men. They had two six inch guns (8 men in a team and the same number in reserve), searchlight crews, observation teams, machine gun crews, a 12-pounder dual (land and air) purpose gun and a Bofors anti-aircraft gun. There was practice firing but never firing 'in anger' whilst he was stationed on the Island.

They were plagued by mosquitoes and because L/Bdr Howell was covered in blotches he was sent to Shaftesbury Hospital. The doctor laughed when he said that he was from Brownsea Island. He was told that he had Brownsea Mosquito poisoning. He did see Mrs Christie and knew that she did not like the troops on the Island. He remembers one occasion when some pigeons (there was a pigeon loft in the Castle grounds and another near the farm) were missing and the soldiers were blamed. A mass parade was called and the officer in charge gave the men a 'dire warning'. From another source those going on home leave usually had a brown paper parcel with them – a peacock killed and taken home to supplement the meat ration.

Mr Murray when he visited the Island in 1976 told Harry Moyle about his wartime memories. He was with 347 Coastal Battery – part of 554 Coast Regiment commanded by Major Tupple from 1940 to November 1943. The troops called Brownsea Island 'Alcatraz' but later on as a German prisoner of war, Mr Murray considered this term most inappropriate. He remembers the Guard Room (now the National Trust reception area) with administration offices above and the present National Trust Coffee Shop as the main messing and ablution centre. He did not mention the Officers' Mess. The cottages near the clock tower were NAAFI buildings and the upstairs were used as billets for the machine gun crews. He confirmed that the Quay Cottages were used as billets for the gun crews but said that Mrs Christie's butler, a Mr Wheeler, and his housekeeper Miss Palmer, lived in the Agent's house. The Farm Cottages were used by the observation crews. John and Mary Hilton lived in a farm cottage and amongst their duties were looking after eight cats 'housed in another cottage'. Before the greenhouses were damaged (the main wall still stands in Middle Street about 500 yards from the Church) they looked after them. The rats fed on the peaches, which were allowed to drop. Mrs Christie lived in the Castle and had a maid Gladys. The Castle, the Castle gardens and the Castle pier were out-of-bounds for the troops. One day several soldiers in 'Army issue' bathing trunks (meaning stark naked) went swimming from the Castle beach and were reported to the Commanding Officer by Mrs Christie, who had seen them through binoculars.

Mr Murray confirmed that the Home Guard came to the Island on duty on Wednesday evenings. They were very popular as they brought over home cooking which the soldiers helped to consume. He remembered that a Mr Johnson commanded the Home Guard (elsewhere Alderman Butler is named as C.O.), and other names he could recall were Hayd, Knight, Harold Beale and Fred Wallace. In 1942 the Island guns were equipped with radar range finders. The anti-invasion plans classified the Island as 'Class A' Strong Point of Defence.

In 1944 Bombardier 'Lofty' Ould was posted to the 347 Coastal Battery (C.O. then was Major Prentice). He told John Barker that he had just returned from Burma. When a local policeman who had not left the U.K. contracted malaria, Lofty Ould was thought to be the carrier. They used the Pottery Pier built by the Army on the western side of the Island. There was a guardroom on the cliffs above the pier. Mrs Christie's son, a Major in the Intelligence Corps was challenged and apprehended when he landed at Maryland one night. He congratulated them on their alertness! All round Maryland there were slit trenches and barbed wire.

Lofty Ould remembers tulips (possibly he means daffodils) being picked by soldiers to take to their girl friends. Mrs Christie opened the Italian Room for them for their 1944 Christmas dinner. A visitor to the Island in 2001 had said that she allowed the troops to hold a service in the Church. An army Captain played the organ. Lofty Ould remembers two employees who came

Lt Commander Vandy, in charge of the harbour and moorings, tackles a difficult task off Brownsea Castle, with the help of local Bolson-built Skylark and Gondolier boats, formerly used for trips round the harbour and Island.

over on the Monday 'rations' boat for the army personnel, and then returned home on the Friday afternoon. The soldiers nicknamed them Bill and Ben. It was thought that they were 'sneaks' informing Mrs Christie what the soldiers were 'up to' on her Island. No Royal Navy personnel were on the Island when Lofty Ould came in 1944. The guns were only fired in practice to calibrate them. They were designed to be mounted on naval ships and when on land with fixed mountings they were unable to compensate for the rise and fall of the tide. The guns were fired towards Studland with sand filled shells. He had been told that peacocks from the Island had been sold in Poole market as turkeys. Gull and duck eggs from the marsh (now the lagoon) were plentiful and supplemented the soldiers' rations. Another soldier had said that Mrs Christie paid soldiers to bury dead peacocks and peahens. This was abused because the soldiers would show some feathers and bones after they had eaten the peacocks!

During 1941 MSNDs (Major Strategic Night Decoys) were set up near 'strategic towns'. Poole with its harbour, factories, high-octane fuel storage and the large cordite factory at Holton Heath a few miles to the west, was one of these strategic towns. A MSND was set up at Arne and another on Brownsea Island. On the Island, Elstree Film Studio technicians helped to design the pyrotechnic devices and Aish & Co, a Poole electrical engineering company, were responsible for the electric ignition of the detonators. In 1992 Mr Alf Keeping who had been employed by Aish & Co told John Barker the details of the Island decoy installation. Another local company, Witchampton Paper

Mills, supplied waste fibre for burning. Most MSNDs were the responsibility of the RAF but on Brownsea Island it was the Navy's responsibility. The decoys had to be at least three quarters of a mile from habitation and were set up near Maryland. To be more realistic a pier was built, roughly where the 'new' Pottery Pier is now, and promises were made to Mrs Christie that it would be demolished after the war. The army personnel at the eastern end of the Island remained on the Island. The authorities wanted Mrs Christie to leave the Island but she steadfastly refused and remained! A few employees living in the farm cottages or on or near the quay at the eastern end of the Island also stayed on the Island.

Alf Keeping went over to the Island in 1942. He remembers passing through fields of daffodils so it was probably in April. There were three types of decoys set up on several sites 'fairly close to the shore' at the western end of the Island. One was to have timber and coal in a lattice of containers which when ignited burnt until the fuel had been exhausted. Another system consisted of large metal troughs with fires underneath. Close by in the hillside were large metal tanks, some containing paraffin and others water. Once paraffin was piped to the heated troughs an intense flare-up started. Water was then released from a tank – like flushing a toilet – which semi-doused the flames. The electrics were installed so that the operator could start the pyrotechnics from a safer distance and created the impression of continuous explosions. The outside of the dugout shelter/control room can still be seen about 300 metres west of the Commemorative Scout Stone. Now it is labelled EWS – Emergency Water Supply. A third type of pyrotechnic to simulate incendiary bombs were open- topped drums sunk into the ground on an open site. These had cordite rings placed in them. 'Flare Bags' filled with a black powder with two wires protruding were connected to the control dugout. All the pyrotechnic systems were set up during the day and a skeleton force left on the Island to control the ignitions. Thunderstorms were a problem as they ignited the systems prematurely and they had to be set up again the next day.

The code name for igniting the decoys was 'Starfish'. It was in operation on the night of 21 – 22 May 1942 when 55 enemy aircraft were plotted on a path towards Poole. The German pathfinders dropped their incendiary bombs to mark the target for the less experienced navigators of the bombers. The fire fighters in Poole rushed to extinguish the fires and the order was given for operation Starfish. For the next 20 minutes 166 tons of bombs were dropped on or near the Island. Only nine tons were dropped on Poole killing five people and injuring others. One can imagine the large number of fatalities, injuries and extensive damage to homes and factories if all the bombs had dropped in Poole. On Brownsea Island there were no injuries to people although the residents that night had a very frightening 20 minutes and the houses at Maryland were badly damaged. A few bomb craters can still be seen on the Island. German reconnaissance planes must have spotted the deception because next time the decoy was ignited the German bombers ignored it.

Barney Chapman replied to a request in 'The Sapper' magazine and gave John Barker details of the Bomb Disposal Unit. They spent 10 days on the Island making the unexploded bombs safe. They nicknamed the Island 'Peacock Island'. 'There were hundreds of peacocks and hens making a hell

Maryland Village damaged during decoy 'STARFISH'.

of a row at night!' The unexploded bombs were made safe and taken to the quay ready to be taken to the mainland. There are three theories to account for quite a large number of unexploded bombs. One theory was that they were made by slave labour from German occupied countries and the detonators were sabotaged. A second theory, they were intended to be unexploded bombs so that normal life or factory production was severely disrupted. Barney Chapman spoke of the third theory that the bombs were dropped from a low height and the ignition fuse became jammed or was inactive. Some of the unexploded bombs could be seen sticking out of the sandy ground. Very few had penetrated more that 3 feet into the ground. The first bomb they dealt with was a 'Herman' weighing 1000 kilograms. It was on its 'belly' half in and half out of the ground and it took a full day to make safe.

Many soldiers had fond memories of the Island. Ex-Sergeant Peter Barleycorn was only on the Island for one week with 347 Battery whilst the regular detachment went for live firing exercises in North Wales. In 1949 whilst on holiday in the area with his wife, he sought permission to land prompted by his wife who had heard so much about Brownsea. Mrs Christie gave permission – details are given in Chapter 5. A crayon sketch of the Church from brothers PW and FJ Overd made in the early 1940s has been presented to the Island and is held in the archives.

Much military and naval activity was witnessed from the Island culminating with 320 vessels leaving the harbour on the 4th June 1944 for the D-Day landings on the French coast. At the end of the war there were few military personnel left on the Island. Barbed wire was dumped in the slit trenches at Maryland before they were filled in. The pier near Maryland was demolished as promised. Mrs Bonham Christie was in sole control of the Island once more.

POST - WAR YEARS
until 1957

I have spoken to several people – some did not wish to be named – who as teenagers went to Brownsea Island. If they had a motor or rowing boat, the unofficial visit to Brownsea Island was a great adventure. In the following weeks, or even months, this was a source of stories shared with their peers. Everyone knew that the Island was guarded by keepers with guns and guard dogs. Some people did not leave the beaches, as the cliffs were sandy and crumbling. Everywhere was overgrown with brambles and bracken and it was said that even the heather was three feet tall. One person said that once you had lost sight of the sea it was easy to get lost. Most of the people I spoke to were male.

In an out-of-the-blue telephone call to one lady, she vividly described her visits to the Island about 44 years ago, for nearly 30 minutes. She pinpointed one night visit on the 8th-9th September 1957 when she was a 'mid-teenager'. She mentioned one girl and eight boys – not all on that particular adventure. They met up in Elgin Woods and went over in an old motorboat, the 'Sunbeam' owned by the Rabett brothers. It was a moonlit night and they landed on the south side of the Island. She still remembers the moonlight glinting on the grass, making it shine a brilliant white. They walked to the church and the doorway to the tower stairway was unlocked. They climbed the stairs and when they peered down into the church the covered van Raalte tomb was like a shrouded dead body. By day and night the Island had a 'spooky' feeling. A Roman coin was found on one occasion. She went onto the Island only a few times because it was so over-grown. On passing the Island quay in a boat, rats could be seen as though they were waiting to be fed. During the wartime, living near Parkstone Yacht Club, her father used to say the rats had swum across from Brownsea Island.

Some had seen deer swimming across to the Island and others admitted picking the daffodils, which were plentiful. Sausages had been cooked on the beach. I was told of those who would swim from the mainland to avoid detection and an expected 'good-hiding' from the keeper. One route was from Hamworthy to Arne and then 'down river' to the Island. Others mentioned stories relating to the Island being exaggerated or fictitious. There was a tremendous sense of curiosity and a lot of bravado attached to anyone who could support a claim of having been there. Rowing across did not then seem

Brownsea Castle 1950.
Mrs Bonham Christie lived alone on the second floor.

too difficult, strenuous or a problem with other vessels using Poole Harbour. The decision to be made was whether to pull up the boat into the undergrowth to avoid detection or to anchor offshore for a quick getaway! Cockle collecting was often included or the more sedate fishing from a boat. Gerry Luff's two daughters remember when, aged about ten years, being left on the beach with their mother whilst their father, a boatman for many years, went cockling. The group on the shore often included their aunt with three or four boys. They saw others on the beach and most of the adults knew each other. Sometimes they would wander inland a short distance to collect fir cones. It was not until they were older that they realised that they should not have been there.

One unofficial visitor – now living in France – assured me that as well as having been down the ladder to the wartime observation post he had slept in the church. His two friends had slept in the cabin of a sailing boat anchored off St Andrew's Bay – off the sea wall of the lagoon/marsh. They had heard him disturb the ground nesting gulls as he left in the evening and that they did not see him until the next morning. Several people who landed reported that

Bullnose Morris.

the 'back-door' of the church was unlocked and that they were able to climb the steps to the church tower. The 'eerie sight' of looking through the windows and grilles to the church aisle below was remembered.

Mr Robert Bonham-Christie remembers meeting his great grandmother in the Castle after the war when he was about seven years old. As she was not very tall he did not find her at all daunting and she was easy to talk to. In fact many have said she was more fond of children than adults. He has memories of her clothes smelling of mothballs and a tin of Cadbury chocolate fingers on a side table. Normally she received visitors in the Music Room of the Castle. Some visitors have spoken of meeting her in the Drawing Room. For the last 20 years of her life she lived in a large bed-sitting room on the second floor. Because of the large number of windows the sun was streaming in most of the day. It had views over parts of Poole, Sandbanks, Studland ferry and towards the Purbecks. She had an enormous brass bedstead. A green parrot lived in a huge brass cage – but it was allowed out of its cage! It had the limited vocabulary of two words 'Hello' and 'Goodbye'. Mrs Bonham Christie lived on a diet consisting mainly of eggs, bread, butter, cheese and milk. For guests she kept bottles of sherry and she did not smoke.

For Robert Bonham-Christie, Brownsea Island was 'a magical place' as a teenager. They had a beach below the Castle to play on, boats to sail, and the whole Island to explore. Later they were able to drive the Bullnose Morris. Every year he spent the eight weeks of school summer holidays with his parents (John and Celia), his younger brother Richard and his younger sister

Rosemary on the Island. They lived in the Villano lit by oil lamps, and used Calor gas for cooking. He has lasting memories of the beauty of the Island, especially at dawn and in the evening. He remembered a rusty hulk blocking the slipway next to the quay for several years. Sometime in the 1950s it was cut up with oxy-acetylene equipment and taken away.

The first year he was holidaying on the Island he was badly bitten by mosquitoes. In the following years they did not bother him, He suspected that he had become immune, for in later years mosquitoes in France did not trouble him either. Deer, pheasants (some from the Marston estate) and peacocks were remembered. Hundreds of noisy peacocks! The peacocks nearly caused a German au pair, employed to look after Richard and Rosemary, to die from drowning. On her first day on the Island she went for a swim and the tide and current were taking her out to sea. Her cries of 'Help' were answered by the peacocks and she could not be heard from the Island. She was rescued. One year there were many rats but in other years Robert Bonham-Christie could not remember seeing any. Myxomatosis seemed to wipe out the rabbits. At the time it was thought that the disease was carried to the Island by deer. Squirrels – red or grey – were not remembered. He does remember his great grandmother feeding rats and rabbits together.

Mrs Bonham Christie's son Robert Arthur served in both the First and Second World Wars. He was keen on horse and greyhound racing and on yachting. Two of his yachts were requisitioned and sunk during the evacuation of Dunkirk. Her great grandson, Robert Bonham-Christie, used to stay with his grandfather (Robert Arthur Bonham Christie) on his boat. His grandfather lived 'down the shore' from the Royal Motor Yacht Club, and he had the best view towards Brownsea Island. His time was spent between the Marston Estate, Poole and long holidays on the French waterways. Robert Bonham-Christie believes that one of the three cars (Fiat, Mercedes, Rolls-Royce) stored on the mainland is now in Beaulieu Motor Museum. He does not remember many of the Island cottages being occupied. George Ogilvy showed him how the gas engine in the Engine House on the quay worked. It had a gigantic flywheel, and was similar to the 'hot plug diesel' at Marston House, which charged accumulators of about 120 cells.

Peter Barleycorn, a Sergeant in the Royal Artillery, spent just one week on Brownsea Island during the Second World War – probably in February 1943, when his detachment stood in for RA batteries for the week when they went for live firing exercises in North Wales. He was billeted in a cottage near the clock tower and remembers seeing rats and being told that fishing was prohibited. He went to many battery sites but Brownsea Island was the one he remembered. Frequently he talked about the Island to his wife, so when they came to Bournemouth his wife suggested that he wrote to Mrs Christie seeking permission to land. He was most surprised to get a reply and to be given permission to land;

'I only received your letter to-day 28th although yours is dated the 26th and we have only one post in a day and one post out both at the same time at 9 o'clock a.m. So although I am replying to this the day I received it, it will not go until tomorrow, Friday morning and I do not expect you will receive it

Mrs Bonham Christie and Poole Pirates.

until Saturday when you say you are returning to London, so you would not be able to visit the Island this time you are in Bournemouth but I will be very pleased for you and your wife to do so next time you are in these parts, if you let me know then and the day you would like to come. Of course the Army and Navy did dreadful destruction to the Island and its buildings, the Army I must say did the most and I have had many work people from a Building Firm trying to repair some of the damage and painting all outside with white paint as before instead of the terrible yellows and blues and green paints they dabbed everywhere often these three colours on one door. The work people have been working here well over a year.'

His next problem was to find a boatman willing to ferry them across. A gamekeeper with a shotgun would not let them land until he had seen the letter, and even then the boatman waited off shore rather than tying up at the quay. He did not see Mrs Christie and commented how the Island was overgrown with brambles.

Some who tried to gain access were denied permission to land. One of these was Peter Scott (later Sir Peter Scott) who was preparing programmes to broadcast on wildlife. She believed that publicity would increase the problem of unwanted visitors. She was most reluctant to allow anyone to land to carry out bird counts. She is reported to have seen a boy, from a Poole school, who was writing a project on wildlife. In 1950 she did allow a surveyor from the Royal Commission on Historical Monuments (England) to visit the church. However a letter dated 12th August begins 'I am trusting that you are now recovered and back on your delectable Island' and this makes me wonder if they may have chosen a date knowing that she was away! However as the church is excluded from her ownership it would be very difficult for her to stop a bone-fide inspection. The letter comments on the woodwork and other church fittings as of unusual interest and confirms that the panelled ceiling to the tower is 'almost certainly one of the six bays of the ceiling from the Great Chamber of Crosby Hall constructed in 1466'. The Scouts tried to arrange, without success, a Golden Jubilee celebration of the movement on the Island in 1957. In 1960 in an outraged letter, Mrs Bonham Christie, written it must be remembered towards the end of her life, expresses her views on Scouts:

"I certainly do not consider it is right to spend money on buildings for Scouts, also my experience is very poor of them. They treat the poor dumb animals who cannot speak nor have no money to defend themselves so cruelly. When younger.....I many times stopped them ill treating without cause older people's dogs and cats, stealing the eggs from the nests of birds, killing with a catapult birds in trees and one of the things Lord Baden Powell started it for was to teach them help and kindness to the dumb creatures. I always call them the wicked little boys groups. PS I hope this is readable. I see so little of what I write and cannot read what I do write." Yet it seems no scouts had been on the Island since 1934!

A reporter in 1959 remarkably gained access and an interview with Mrs Bonham Christie, who he described as 'The Queen of Silence.' He was 'a Poole boy with an interest in local history', Warren Davis, who was a reporter on the then Poole and Dorset Herald. (He later became Press officer with the National Trust after it acquired the island.) In the resulting article he foreshadowed 'that the frustrated sightseers who now condemn the owner for so jealously guarding the island's privacy will one day praise her for her wisdom.' Even more presciently he wrote, 'One can but guess what 95-yr old Mrs Bonham Christie has willed for her mysterious sanctuary, where only the macabre cry of peacocks stabs the heavy silence of the woods'. 'Will it become a national park, as the Herald suggested in 1939, a holiday playground with chalets in the shrubbery or a green retreat for ornithologists?'

In a report in the Bournemouth Evening Echo, November 1957, a councillor of Wareham and Purbeck Rural District Council commented, 'Instead of a wilderness infested with vermin of every description we have found a Garden of Eden. Instead of being a blot on our escutcheon it is a gem in our crown'. He was commenting on a report from the Senior Public Health Officer. The report stated that water supplies were adequate and the sewage disposal plant was functioning satisfactorily. In the same report Pest Officers authoritatively stated that there was 'no evidence whatsoever to indicate the presence of rats, mice, rabbits or any other vermin'. The report continued, 'The cottages on the Island were generally in a sound structural condition', but I suspect that the report did not include the derelict cottages at Maryland. At a previous meeting the Council was told that other than the Castle only two of the fifteen habitable buildings were permanently occupied.

It is said that Mrs Christie was delighted to receive the few visitors, particularly children, she allowed into the Castle. The invited visitors would be received in the Castle drawing room. Mrs Christie herself, not a maid, would serve refreshments. One lady who went frequently with her young nephew told me that they had chocolate cake 'sent down from London'. When Mrs Christie was out of the room the nephew would hide under one of the tiger skin rugs. These rugs may have been included in the original purchase. I cannot imagine that they were brought from Marston but nevertheless I am surprised that they were still to be seen.

Mrs Iris Gray remembers being invited to afternoon tea at the Castle in 1949 or 1950 after her mother, Mrs Dingley, had visited Mrs Bonham Christie in Strathallan Nursing Home, where she was recovering from an arm or leg injury. Iris Gray and her mother went by rowing boat from Sandbanks. They were surprised that Mrs Bonham Christie was living alone in the Castle, did not have servants, and prepared and served the tea and Swiss rolls herself. Most of the furniture was covered in dust sheets. Orange peel was behind some of the chairs and Mrs Bonham Christie explained that this was to check that the cleaner was doing her job! She let it be known she did not wish to answer questions about the history of the Castle.

Derek Loader remembers large peacock feathers decorating her room.

In 1948 Bill Parsons worked in the Castle as an apprentice plumber. In 1949 he worked at the Villa and on the Island water supply. Work was being carried out on a Castle wall – possibly damaged by practice firing of the 6-inch guns situated nearby in the Second World War. Lamberts, the builders, had six workers on the Island who had to reconstruct an end wall of the Castle. The plumbers, from G N Haydon Ltd, had to remove the central heating pipes and replace them when the bricklayers and stonemasons had completed the wall. They were taken across at 8 am and usually reached the Island by 8.30 am. They were not allowed to start work at the Castle until 10 am. Mrs Christie, 83 years old in 1948, did not go to bed until the early hours of the morning and did not wish to be disturbed before 10 am. She was living in just one large room in the Castle and remained in the room when the workmen were working in it. In the morning she was still in bed, 'a gigantic bed', drinking a cup of tea brought in by George Ogilvy. Bill Parsons often returned the tray to the kitchen. At noon the workmen had to take their lunch and when they returned at 1 pm, Mrs Christie was dressed sitting in a chair in the corner of the room. Dressed in black she looked 'just like Queen Victoria'. There was no conversation between Mrs Christie and the workers. Occasionally she would say, 'Will you come and have a look at this?' or 'Where are you working now? - I want to see what you are doing'. She had a stick and walked very slowly, particularly on the stairs. She had a dog, which may have been a breed similar to a Chow. It had a 'massive great sore' across its back. Cream was rubbed into the sore leaving an awful smell in the room. There was some expensive looking furniture but it was 'very tatty'. The carpet was full of holes. In every other room the furniture was stacked in the middle of the room and covered with green and white or red and white check cloths. On the carpets by the legs of the furniture were little piles of woodworm dust.

The contractors spent some time getting the whole heating system working in the Castle. The boilers, heated by burning timber, were in the basement. At high tide the basement would flood, as the pumps were not working. When a leak was found the whole system had to be drained, the leak mended and the radiators refilled. At the end of September 1948 the heating system was working. Mrs Christie went to every room to check that the radiators were hot. Then the whole system was completely drained! The cold-water storage tanks in the roof were cut out and replaced by 'bolt-together tanks'. Drinking water was piped to the Castle and pumped up to the storage tanks. The Water Company had to send a surveyor to trace the pipes under the cellar. All the keys for the Castle were tagged and hung in a small room. When a storeroom under an arched doorway was opened 'hundreds and hundreds' of bottles of wine were seen. Most of the corks in the bottles had deteriorated or had been chewed by rats, although a few seemed intact. On the floor were two boxes containing bottles of champagne. In the key room were about a dozen rusty shotguns confiscated by George Ogilvy. When he saw a poachers' boat he would drop anchor and await their return. As an alternative to prosecution they would hand over their shotguns.

The Island boatman collected the workmen at 8 am from a jetty – at Branksea, Mrs Christie's Sandbanks house. The workers left their bicycles in the barn near the three cars. The cars seemed in good condition but did not appear to be used. George Ogilvy (known as George to the workmen) was an interesting character. It was said that in the Second World War he was in the Merchant Navy and was captured by the German battleship Scharnhorst and transferred to the prison ship Altmark. Someone else had thought that he had been a Japanese prisoner of war. He had been affected by his wartime experiences and was quick to take offence, so the workers were careful what they said to him. On a couple of occasions he had become bad tempered and had refused, at first, to take them back to the mainland. Towards the end of their time on the Island the plumbers became friendly with him and had been invited to his cottage (next to the engine shed) for a cup of tea. He drove the 1908 'Dodge type' lorry with wooden wheels and solid tyres – 'a beautiful thing'. It used to start at the first swing of the cranking handle every time. There was a modern fire tender on the Island, which looked out of place when towed by the ancient lorry.

Neither of the two employees on the Island had wives. Mannings the gamekeeper was never called by his first name and should not be confused with John (Hugh) Manning who came to the Island late in 1957. Mannings lived in one of the three cottages near the South Shore. Mrs Christie did not know that his wirehaired terrier was good at catching rabbits! In front of the Castle were three very big circular wooden trays. Every day Mannings would fill them with food – biscuits, bread etc. for the peacocks, rabbits, pheasants, rats and rabbits, all feeding together. Bill Parsons was told that there were 60 to 70 peacocks at the beginning of the Second World War and only about six at the end of the war. Red Squirrels were not noticed but he thought that most of the trees on the North side of the Island had herons' nests in them. Hundreds of broken eggshells were on the ground, from herons or ground nesting gulls. There were two cows and a horse on the Island when the contractors first went there in 1948. The cows could not bend their front legs and used to hop instead of walking. They were in a poor condition. When the horse died the builders dug a grave on the edge of the marsh. Bill Parsons thought that both cows died whilst he was working on the island – later reports indicate just one died. The rats were not afraid of people – they had to be almost pushed out of the way as the workers went across the Castle gardens. Many live rats were found when the workers were clearing out the Castle roof space, but mosquitoes were not a problem.

Often the plumber and his apprentice had to wait for the bricklayers to complete a section of wall. They took advantage of this spare time to explore the 'forbidden Island'. The farm building doors were not locked. In one small outhouse was a dogcart – a baby carriage decorated with black lace hangings. The stables (now demolished) looked as though no one had been in them for years. There was a 'Marie Celeste' atmosphere with leathers, straps and saddles hanging from posts and falling to pieces. In the cowshed next door, the cows' names still marked the stalls. Between the farm and the church the field was overgrown with gorse and brambles. They had to beat and cut their way through them. The church door was shut but not locked. The marriage register, not used since 1924, was in the lectern. A narrow path was kept clear by the side of the church, now called Middle Street. They could not get far along this path and at first thought that there was only one lake on the Island. 'Masses and masses' of ducks were seen on the second lake. Both East and West Lakes are in the Reserve now. They ate their sandwiches and did their pipe cutting in the old school room. They renovated the heating system in the rambling house known to the builders as the Manor. This was the Villa, which is now the home of the Dorset Wildlife Reserve Warden. The house was in an 'awful condition and alive with rats'. Again the heating system was left drained and the house left unoccupied and locked up. The greenhouses along Middle Street were falling down. The plumbers were particularly interested in the pipe work, which in 2002 can still be seen. Water tanks had rusted through. Vines were still there and growing through the broken glass.

In 1949 the water pipes supplying the Castle with fresh water had to be cleared of silt. The water came from the lakes. Two labourers from Lamberts had to cut their way through under-growth and rhododendrons, dig a trench for about 25 yards to expose the pipe. The plumbers cut out the section of pipe to clear it and then the pipe was replaced and the trench was filled. This was continued from the Lakes to the Castle.

Each Tuesday was a special day. George Ogilvy would go late in the morning to ferry to the Island the Vicar of St Peter's Church, a clock winder and a cooked dinner. The dinner had been cooked at the mainland house, 'Branksea'. Sometimes a relative – possibly grandson John Bonham-

Christie – would come across as well. The clock winder was thought to spend the rest of the day in the clock tower. As the clock would not take long to wind, what he did until the return at 5 pm was, and is, a mystery. There is a suspicion that this could have been a joke story told to the young apprentice but the winder was not seen elsewhere. The Vicar would spend the afternoon with Mrs Christie.

There was another strange story concerning the cooked lunch. Definitely this was not a joke as Bill Parsons saw it happen. The dinner/lunch came wrapped in cloths to keep it warm and it was taken to the 'massive' Castle kitchen. Rats were there and others -'not one or two, but dozens' - could be

Edward Chubb checks the daffodils in 1956

seen peering into the kitchen window. The meal was placed on the kitchen table and covered with a wire cage. Mrs Christie would eat it stone cold on Thursday. Bill Parsons noted that this was a regular procedure – the meal brought over hot on Tuesday and eaten cold on Thursday. He is sure of this as he had carried the meal to the kitchen on a Tuesday and had seen it uneaten on the Wednesday. On Thursday there were empty plates!

A 'well known gypsy' family of father and two or three sons used to cross to the Island to pick daffodils. As George Ogilvy took them across it was assumed that they had permission from Mrs Christie. When they returned with the construction workers at 5 pm they carried big wicker baskets containing 'thousands and thousands' of daffodils. Dot Cooke, who as Dot Boyt, remembers picking daffodils on the Island with other members of her family for her uncle Edward Chubb of Chubb Nurseries in 1955 and 1956. 98-year-old Mrs Gladys Boyt, Dot's mother, remembered the work and believed that Mr Dibben was also organising daffodil pickers at that time. The daffodils were picked in the field near Rose Cottage. The field now known as the Daffodil Field still produces the daffodils but the deer, peacocks and rabbits destroy many of the buds. The daffodils were sent to London as well as being sold locally. Nobody was seen on patrol. One cow was photographed but it did not take any notice of the pickers. Coincidentally, Dot and Warwick Cooke came to live on the Island and work for the National Trust in 1968 and reported that the crane on the quay was still in use then.

Miss Blackmore, whose father had been Water Postman, calling at Brownsea Island from 1919 to 1924 – but that is another story – told me that Miss Baker of Paynes in Poole High Street had yearly contracts with Mrs

Christie to pick daffodils. This she did for about five years possibly from 1957 to 1961. Miss Blackmore took photographs of the pickers in a 'sea of yellow daffodils' in 1957. Miss Baker became quite friendly with Mrs Christie and some Island plant pots she gave to her were passed to Miss Blackmore and are now back on the Island, though damaged by frost. Miss Blackmore remembers Mr and Mrs Capel, working for Mrs Christie and living on the Island. Weekly they went shopping for Mrs Christie. She also visited them when they moved to the Marston estate after Mrs Christie died.

The sea walls from the Castle, past the Quay Cottages onto the wall protecting the reclaimed (in 1853) St Andrew's Bay, were kept in a good state of repair. Strengthening the piers was remembered by 97 years old Mr Futcher, a diver. In the early 1950s he worked with six others over two long periods of time repairing and strengthening the two piers at the Castle and near the Quay cottages. He remembered their launch picking up a worker, possibly Bill Baker as George Loader would only be crossing at weekends, who used to cut wood to burn. Much of the wood was 'too good to burn' and he made himself a mallet out of a piece of beech. As they passed the wall by the marsh, hundreds of birds would fly up and 'deafen us' with their cries. They would wave to Billy Cotton as they passed his boat 'Wakey Wakey', named after his radio show. They took over much of the gravel and cement needed and a barge brought over materials too difficult for the launch to carry. Their materials were stored in empty cottages. Again rats were seen. He saw one cow and had heard there was another on the Island. The cow was 'skin and bone' and could only hobble along. A vet came over while they were there and told them that there was nothing he could do, 'just old age and they had not been to bull'.

Maurice Cartridge's father Harry (1899-1992) was skipper of Captain Christie's (Mrs Christie's son) 55-foot yacht 'Fionola' from 1949. Often Maurice would accompany his father when Captain Christie visited his mother – only by appointment. When Captain Christie went to the Castle, Maurice Cartridge and his father would go onto the Island. When Maurice Cartridge was an apprentice with the boat builders, R A Newmans, he worked with Alfie Dean, who was born on Brownsea Island and had lived at Maryland. Several generations of the Dean family had lived and worked on the Island. Alfie had tried to get permission from Mrs Christie to visit his parents' grave in the churchyard but this had been refused. From time to time Maurice Cartridge would struggle through the brambles and rhododendrons to make sure the grave was kept in good order.

Captain Christie and his family would spend much of the summer cruising on the French waterways. Harry Cartridge's wife would accompany him to act as stewardess. Amongst the rest of the crew was Frank Holdsworth, the engineer. Captain Christie owned a bungalow, The Moorings, near Salterns Marina. A tender was kept at Poole Harbour Yacht Club at Salterns. 'Fionola' was anchored in Brownsea Roads. At the old coaching stable in Grasmere Road (i.e. at the 'Branksea' house) yacht spares and anything for the Island were left. Maurice Cartridge had never met Mrs Christie or been inside the Castle. He had seen her many times on the Castle terrace feeding 'umpteen rats'. She was wearing a long black dress and it looked as though a black carpet was wrapped around her. Bill Baker who lived on the mainland was

Overgrown St Mary's Church 1950's.

the Island boatman, odd job man and lorry driver. Bill Baker would catch gigantic conger eels off the quay pier. They were so long – seven or eight feet – that he would hang them from the carpenters shop pulley to skin them. It was said that an eel bit right through a diver's suit when he was repairing the windmill. A huge windmill roughly where the wind pump is now, estimated at 30 or 40 feet across, used to pump out water from the marsh area, now the Lagoon. John Christie stayed, mainly in the summer, with his family at the Villano. He owned 'Diligence of Marston' built at Harry Newman's shipyard. A Mr Stone who had been Mrs Christie's chauffeur lived at 'Branksea' on the mainland.

As well as Mr Dibben's daffodil-picking contract, it was believed that a lady named Buckmaster from the Peoples' Florist had a contract for several years. Mrs Christie sent over a huge bunch of daffodils for the tables at the reception when Maurice Cartridge married Jo Sydenham.

Two cows would be seen leaning against a tree near the church waiting for Bill Baker to bring their daily feed of hay. Bill Baker felt that they should have been put down some years before. In the church, Charles van Raalte's memorial was covered with a cloth so thin that it was like tissue paper. Once lead was stolen from the roof of the church and some of the stonework around the tower was pushed off. This damaged some of the gravestones including Alfie Dean's parents' gravestone, and Harry Cartridge arranged for the repairs to be made.

Derek Loader told me that his grandfather David started working at weekends on the Island sometime after the war. Later his father George used

Overgrown Churchyard.

to join him. Later still his mother Lotty (Charlotte) used to go over, and Derek remembers going to the Island with them around 1952 – the year many rabbits died of myxomatosis – as a school boy 'still in short trousers'. He remembers the boat being rowed through ice so it may have been a very cold winter earlier than 1952. Initially they went over on Saturdays and Sundays and eventually stayed overnight in the cottage on the right hand side of the engine house.

Derek Loader used to go over until sometime in 1961, a few months after Mrs Christie died. He remembers Bill Baker as the handyman and George Ogilvy – confirming previous descriptions that he looked like George Formby. Bill Baker used to come over daily, catching a bus from Hamworthy to Sandbanks. He was paid £1 a day. On Christmas Day, with no buses running, he would row from Hamworthy. As a special treat Mrs Christie let him leave at 2 pm that day! Other Island workers' names remembered were John Stacey and his wife and Mr McCabe but they were not employed for long. Most of the time, other than Mrs Christie, George Ogilvy was the only resident. George Ogilvy used to row the boat across from Sandbanks. One year – possibly 1947 – he had to row through ice. George Ogilvy was quite an unusual character. Derek Loader understood that he had been a Japanese prisoner of war and that he had been tortured. This included removing his fingernails. He did not talk about it but he had difficulty with picking up money. He used to play in a dance band at the Haven Hotel. Preparing for a Saturday night performance he would change and wear patent leather shoes. He would then run down the ramp by the side of the island pier into the water, jump into his boat and row across to Sandbanks. Others reported that he used to be seen playing a violin in the Island Quay. In his living room there was a sea scene painted around the walls (due to renovations there is no trace of this). One day a five-gallon drum with skull and crossbones painted on it was washed up on the beach near Rose Cottage. George charged it with a branch and then beat it. Derek Loader and his father did not stop nearby! It was a smoke canister but could have contained very dangerous chemicals.

The main job for the Loader menfolk was to clear pathways, make firebreaks and cut timber for the Castle boilers. George Loader would travel to Sandbanks on the bus with a large crosscut saw wrapped in sacking around him. On the Island, young Derek would be covered in sacking to dissuade the mosquitoes from biting his bare legs. The mosquitoes were 'massive and blood would squirt out from them when squashed'. In the Castle boiler house there were two boilers. Water came from the lakes and went through some heather beds in the Castle grounds to purify it. There was a two-stroke water-cooled Lister engine, which pumped the water up to the tanks in the roof. The Quay Cottages collected their water from a well in their communal gardens. Mrs Christie was living in one room in the Castle. She used the back stairs to bring down Jinnie, a little black and white terrier. The dog was deaf and to attract its attention they would clap their hands.

Derek Loader seldom went to Mrs Christie's room. She used to talk to him. He remembers cleaning out the parrot cage for her. Once a year Mrs Christie gave the Loader family a treat. George Ogilvy was told to give them a boat trip round the Island! Mrs Christie made a fuss of her pets. Before Jinnie, she had a brown Golden Spaniel, which had belonged to George Ogilvy. A rat was seldom seen. There were 'hundreds' of peacocks. Eggs were collected from the white geese for Mrs Christie to cook. The geese could not fly and were fed at the farm. Derek Loader believed that bread was brought to the Island by the water postman. When Mr and Mrs Capel came to live and work on the Island, Mrs Capel would take 'cooked tripe and chiplings' to Mrs Christie. The Castle kitchens were 'massive', with all sizes of copper pots – possibly from the van Raalte ownership – hanging on the walls. Mrs Christie did not use these kitchens but had a little oil heater for cooking in her room. She did not eat much. One of Mrs Christie's sayings was 'Never take what you cannot give back', hence her views on animals and birds. Two cows fed by Bill Baker were seen on the Island. The last one, Edith, was trapped in a bog, and, although the fire brigade came over to try to release it, it died and was buried there. It was thought to be over 36 years old.

Mrs Christie seemed to be up 'half the night'. Mrs Loader would tidy up in the Castle, often her husband would have to go to the Castle at 2 or 3 am to remind them that it was bedtime! On a Sunday, George Ogilvy would get upset because he had to wait after 3.30 pm for Mrs Christie to finish chatting to Mrs Loader.

Mr George Loader worked as a bricklayer five days a week. Some of his £1 a day pay on Brownsea Island would be required for the four bus journeys a day getting to and from Sandbanks. On the Island, clearing paths was very tedious. Only about ten feet a day was cleared as the undergrowth, brambles and rhododendrons were so thick. The logs for the boiler fires were cut mainly from the 1934 fire-damaged trees. They were cut into three-foot lengths and taken by a four-wheeled truck to the Castle. When the dog Bryn came to the Island (see Chapter 6) he would be waiting for them on the quay and would spend the day with them. Eventually he would watch them leave at the end of the day. When the truck carrying the wood was travelling fast down Brown Hill (the slope near the farm) he would run alongside the truck barking excitedly. Near the tumbledown Seymer's Cottage, Derek Loader saw his only red squirrel on the Island in about ten years and regrettably it was dead. At Maryland there was a deep well. Most of the unwelcome visitors appeared to land at this end of the Island but left when shouted at! Derek Loader spent many hours down in the Second World War Royal Artillery observation post. He had been told that Americans had been billeted in the Villa during the war and had buried all the equipment they could not take with them – including a jeep! Often on Saturday evenings he dug holes near the Villa without success.

Mrs Christie offered George Loader the three cars on the mainland for £100 each, the Rolls Royce having only 145 miles on the clock. Sometime afterwards he regretted that he had not purchased them! I have been told that the Rolls Royce "Brownsea" – all early Rolls Royces have names – was sold for £300,000 in 2002.

Her Final Years

1957-1961

Most of the information in this chapter is based on the interviews with John (Hugh) Manning and Barry Guest who were appointed boatman/handyman/patrolman on Brownsea Island in 1957 (or late 1956 until 1960) and October 1960 respectively. Other than the boatman the only other permanent residents were Mr and Mrs Capel. The Loader family came over at weekends. In 1957 Mrs Christie was 92 years old, still alert, still taking on the authorities she disagreed with, and still preserving the Island for Nature not Humans. Other than clearing gutters, very little work was done to the Castle or the cottages in this period.

Unmarried, John Manning was in his early 20's when appointed. He saw the advertisement in the Western Daily News. She called him to interview by letter. This letter had to be shown to a boatman at Sandbanks before the boatman would take him across. No boatman was employed by Mrs Christie at that time; Mrs Christie interviewed him in the Castle drawing room. He remembered that she questioned him 'from A to X' and stared at him with beady eyes as though she was reading his mind. In his opinion, she was a very astute lady. Although it was not spelt out he felt that if he told her a lie during the employment he would get instant dismissal. Early in his employment this was put to the test. He had bought a dingy with an outboard motor for himself, as the Island launch was difficult to moor and anchor. Once a week he went to Sainsbury's in Bournemouth to shop for Mrs Christie and himself. Being young and not fully organised he needed some more food before the weekly shopping day. He jumped into his dingy and went to the mainland. The next time he saw Mrs Christie she questioned him about leaving the Island. He told her that he had been shopping and he had paid for the dingy and petrol. She insisted that he restricted his mainland visits to one a week! He found a canoe in a storeroom and he took it to the lakes. One day a reporter 'sneaked' on to the Island. The newspaper report mentioned the canoe seen on the lake. Mrs Christie read the newspaper and questioned him about it. She was satisfied with his answer that he wanted to check that there was not an injured bird on the island on the lake.

He soon realised Mrs Christie did not want any animals killed. Soon after he arrived he saw a mouse on the Castle stairs. When he asked her what bait he should use to catch it, he was told to leave food for it daily! Maize was bought for the peacocks. He did not see any rats in the time he was there – this agreed with the Purbeck District report in Chapter 5. He was told, incorrectly, that all the rats had left the Island in 1934 at the time of the fire. To help him with his Island patrol work he brought a dog, Bryn, to the Island. One day the dog disturbed a hornets' nest, stinging the dog and badly stinging John Manning. He remembers thinking he was going to die. There was no phone on the Island, as it had been disconnected many years previously, so he managed to treat himself successfully with bicarbonate of soda and vinegar mixture. He had seen both red squirrels and a few grey ones on the Island. A lot of rabbits were seen and one black tame rabbit. On the quay was a large cage used to allow injured birds and animals to recover and to be set free again.

The water postman (Harry Reeves' name has been mentioned as one of them) called six days a week including Christmas Day. Even if there was no mail to deliver, the post-box, still on the quay, had to be emptied. Nowadays the postman goes on an early National Trust ferry from Sandbanks. In the 1950s, and earlier, the postman also brought over newspapers, milk, bread and other items, if ordered. For Bryn and the Capel's dog Freddie, the postman would bring a couple of bones. The dogs would watch for his boat approaching from Poole and then they would dash excitedly to await his arrival on the quay.

John Manning was left to decide his own pattern of work. As time went on he enjoyed working on the Island so much that the weekly shopping expedition became a chore. Having been an engineer in the navy he particularly enjoyed being a maintenance engineer on the Island. He mentions a Petters pump used to pump water up to the tanks in the Castle. There was an indicator on the outside Castle wall to show the level of water in the tanks. Mrs Christie did not use a lot of water and it only needed pumping about once a week. At one time the water flow from the lakes became very weak. Luckily the flow to a manhole in the Church Field was stronger so John Manning connected a hose to bypass the clogged section. He disputed the heather filter beds mentioned in Chapter 5. He remembered coke being used, perhaps in conjunction with heather. It had to be raked and the collected scum removed, and occasionally the coke had to be renewed.

All the cooking done by Mrs Christie was on a very primitive little oil stove in her room. She washed in cold water, 'her skin was like peaches'. She had a bathroom adjacent to her room where she did her washing. There were several wardrobes in her room. One day John Manning went to see her and noticed one wardrobe mirror was covered with wet handkerchiefs. Mrs Christie saw his look of surprise and explained that after washing they were placed against the mirror to dry. By this method they dried without creasing and hence did not need ironing.

John Manning lived in the Carpenter's Cottage, which is next to the present Reception Area. After about a year his parents joined him and his father was employed to clear the Castle gardens. The Quay Cottages had had a cable connecting one electric light bulb in each cottage to the electricity supply generated in the engine house. John Manning reconnected it. There

The pump on the sea wall. The wind-pumps to drain the lagoon fell into disrepair and created a marsh.

had been a coke-fired generator and a new engine had been installed between the Carpenters Cottage and the other Quay Cottages. It charged glass accumulators resting on slate beds. It used 'gallons and gallons' of distilled water, three or four big glass carboys being brought over at a time. If the engine was not started correctly there was 'an almighty kick-back'. John Manning still has the burn mark inflicted during early days on the Island. The electricity produced was for the Castle. As well as for lighting, it powered the lift. Mrs Christie had to use the lift as her mobility problems became severe.

Another engineering problem he solved was to get the large windmill working to pump out water draining from the Island into the marshes. It worked well and the water level dropped so much that an unexploded bomb was found! Later an army detachment blew it up. The bullnose Morris was on blocks in the farm buildings. He got it working and used it on the paths that were wide enough to take it. The old 'magneto drive and solid tyred' Ford (or possibly the Selden) lorry was very temperamental as the magneto was 'hit and miss'.

Pay was poor – Mrs Christie explained that it had to be below the tax threshold so she did not have to involve the tax authorities. She claimed that she should not be liable for tax and had salvage rights in Poole Harbour under a Royal Charter granted by Henry VIII in the 16th century. When she was in hospital, her grandson John came to look after her affairs. When faced with a tax 'final demand' he paid up and from that day Mrs Christie had to pay tax. For some months John Manning took cheques for each month to the bank to settle tax debts totalling £7,000.

His dog Bryn was a good companion for John Manning particularly when dealing with aggressive poachers. He knew he was vulnerable on the deserted parts of the Island so any boats anchored just off the shore with no occupants were towed to the quay. Then with Bryn by his side, he would negotiate the handing over. When John Manning's boat was left at Sandbanks, Bryn would 'Stay!' and guard it until his return, sometimes over two hours later. When Bryn joined him in the boat off the Island quay he would take a running jump, each time landing in the boat. The problem was when fishermen were fishing, legally, off the quay he would join them by the same method, nearly capsizing their boats. One night in 1960 when checking and locking up the Castle for the night, he came across five intruders aged 20 to 25 years, in the Castle. With Bryn on guard, they were held in a room whilst John Manning went to Sandbanks to summon the police. Later the police were brought over by a launch from the Royal Motor Yacht Club. The intruders claimed that they thought the Castle was deserted. They also said one of the rooms was like a 'musty Aladdin's Cave piled high with all sorts of strange things'. As the intruders had not caused any problems, Mrs Christie did not prosecute them. She noted that Bryn was an asset and put him on the 'pay roll' i.e. she paid for his food. Up until then, the ever-hungry Bryn had cost John Manning a large proportion of his pay in dog food. Later when John Manning left the Island, Mrs Christie insisted that Bryn remained.

In spite of the age difference, John Manning found Mrs Christie interesting to talk to. After a time, she changed from addressing him as 'Mr Manning' to 'John'. Sometimes she would keep him chatting for two hours or more. He remembers her saying that her father's bank was the foundation of the Rothschild millions, implying that the Rothschild took over her father's bank. John Manning was sorry to leave the Island but the pay was poor and the career prospects were limited. He returned to the Island inn 1985 when his second marriage to Diana was blessed in the Church and their marriage vows were renewed there in 1995.

Vivian and Beatrice Capel lived on the quay from about 1955 to 1961. Mrs Capel tidied up for Mrs Christie and did some cooking for her. She had told her daughter-in-law (Mrs Stooks) that sometimes Mrs Christie was in the Castle cellars surrounded by old papers and rags. She would call the rats and share her dinner with them. Mr Capel was a keeper on the Island. He had a beard and was nicknamed 'The Bird Man of Brownsea' by the local press. They were country folk and helped the young boatman to settle into Island life. Mrs Capel was known as Auntie Bea and it was said that she had calming and even healing powers for humans and animals. They were both keen to look after injured birds and animals. John Manning was able to repay their kindness one Christmas time when their son, Gerry Stooks, was rowing across in stormy

Mrs Bonham Christie - 1950's.

seas. John Manning noticed that the boat was being swamped and he took out the Island launch to take him in tow.

In November 1960, the 95-year-old Mrs Christie wrote to her doctor, Dr Burstal; 'The club put their launch away in September, and has no launch running again until Whitsunday and I have just got a boatman, but my launch is being repainted and overhauled after its long rest.

But I am not requiring any doctors visits as my sling can remain and I certainly am not going to go on changing it now. I am well over 95 if I can last on for the few years I have only got remaining.

I have been in my bedroom and lived on the same floor as my bedroom since I last saw you as my leg I told you last week has prevented me going about and just down stairs and my leg is now getting much better, I told you I had a bad leg last time you were here.

I hope you keep well this shocking weather but the government and scientists evidently continue their interferences with the sky clouds and moon etc! So they are the reason for this shocking weather and dreadful floods etc.'

The banister on the Castle stairs finishes before the lowest stair tread. Sometime earlier that year, Mrs Christie had fallen on the last step and had broken her wrist. The sea was too rough to take her off the Island. The doctor came across and he was going to give her a pain killing injection. She refused it, saying, 'You experiment on animals to get these things made'. She was taken to hospital the next day but had sat up all night alone with severe pain.

The new boatman mentioned in the letter was Barry Guest. He had been at sea and wrote to Mrs Christie during a period in hospital, as he wanted a temporary break from the Merchant Navy. She wrote some long rambling letters to him, including the problems of paying super-tax. From a letter, he assumed that he had been offered the job as boatman. When he arrived on the Island, ferried by the Water Postman, he found out that she had not yet decided to appoint him. However she did take him on, but the pay was only £5 a week. Several times Barry Guest extended his temporary employment on the Island and now, over 40 years later, is still there as the National Trust Property Manager.

When appointed, Barry Guest was just over 20 years old. He lived in the School House initially. On the quay at weekends, the Loader family had the cottage to the right of the engine house. Mr & Mrs Capel used the next cottage and a Mr & Mrs Pidgeon had the third cottage for a short time. When they left,

Barry Guest used it. The cottages were not supposed to have electricity but the lead was run through to give each a light downstairs. There was no mains electricity and the Island dynamo produced a 110 volts supply for the Castle. The cottages each had one water tap downstairs – previously I had been told that water came from a well, so this may refer to the period after 1961. There was a 'Raeburn' in each cottage mainly fuelled by wood. When the National Trust took over, coal was used. Calor gas cylinders, purchased from the Royal Motor Yacht Club, were used for cooking and each cylinder lasted about a month.

In 1960, Mrs Christie was 95 years old and still living alone in one room of the Castle. Other than a cooked meal from Mrs Capel, she lived mainly on bread, butter and boiled eggs. She had a primitive camping stove set up in the middle of her room. It consisted of an open tin with methylated spirits in it. 'A horrendous situation when it is considered now' says Barry Guest. An egg boiled dry once and left a terrible smell for several days. She was keen to talk and he would spend up to three hours with her. She knew of many of the stories the press had concocted about her and was not concerned by them. She would laugh when repeating some of the stories. She said that it was too costly to have scientists calling as they would have to be given lunch. She made a great fuss of Bryn, now looked after by Barry Guest. Before taking him into the Castle, his collar would be removed and his fur brushed so Mrs Christie did not notice that he had worn a collar. In the Castle he would bound up the stairs, into her room and would literally jump onto her. Barry Guest was always worried that he would injure her.

Several times the doctor, John Christie and his wife Celia, tried to persuade Mrs Christie to go into a Nursing Home on the mainland. Her stock answer was 'Jerry (i.e. Germans) could not force me to leave my Island and neither are you'. However on the 28th April 1961 she was so ill that, in a wheelchair, she was ferried to the mainland, assisted by St John's Ambulance. Determined to the end, she died before nightfall and so did not spend her last night away from the Island she loved.

AFTER 1961

Mrs Bonham Christie left 40% of her money to her son, Robert Bonham Christie, and 60% of her money and Brownsea Island to her grandson John Bonham Christie. The freely disposable assets were at first valued at £263,942 net, including a valuation for the Island. However taking into account the Trust Fund and the Marston Estate it was estimated that over £750,000 was involved. Mr Bonham Christie was reported as saying that his grandmother's income had come from a family trust, and the Island might have to be sold to pay the death duties. However there was a wish – not a condition – that the Island should be maintained as a bird and animal sanctuary.

John Bonham Christie, his wife Celia and the three children – Robert, Richard and Rosemary – came to live in the Villano, which until then had been their holiday residence. After the death of Mrs Bonham Christie there was considerable pressure from sightseers. Over the years most – but not all – had refrained from landing. It was pointed out that it was a private estate and if it were on the mainland it would have a high wall surrounding it. On the Island

The pottery manager's house, built in the 1870's, was adjacent to Baden Powell's 1907 experimental camp.

Carts not used since 1927 found in an isolated barn. Renovated by N.T. volunteers and on display from 2002.

John Bonham Christie announced to a group of invited reporters and photographers that occasionally he would consider letting selected parties land with authorised guides. The newspapers were full of stories of the last 34 years and they repeated many of the errors and exaggerations made in that period. John Bonham Christie said that the sea wall and the Castle were in good repair and it would have been pointless to repair the cottages at Maryland. Likewise the cottage near the area used at the first experimental scout camp had been badly damaged during the war. Readers who have had to clear out a property after an elderly relative has died will have faced the problem of what to keep, what to sell and what has to be dumped. John Bonham Christie had all this in mammoth proportions, with the added difficulty of transport across the sea. One room of the Castle was filled with saleable items including a 'gigantic' chandelier. It is thought that only £200 was offered for everything in the room. There was even a mantrap, which cut through a broom handle when tested by Derek Loader. One can only wonder when, and by whom, it was brought to the Island – and for what reason! Many journeys were made to rubbish dumps on the Island. John Christie told Barry Guest, Mr & Mrs Capel and the Loader family to take whatever they wanted from the truck before it made its many journeys to the dump. A lot of the contents had been left when Mrs van Raalte had left the Island. Barry Guest remembers trying on a green coat with tails. Was it worn by a coachman, a manservant, or by one of the beaters in the early 20th century? The estate band uniforms, unused since 1925, were taken from the carpenter's shop and buried – except for one jacket. The late Mrs Beryl Parkyn, a voluntary warden, retrieved the jacket, and now it is preserved, in very good condition, at Dorset County Museum.

John Bonham Christie was worried that too many visitors or a fire, as in 1934, would damage the Island his great grandmother had protected. Only three employees, the overgrown jungle, and unsafe sandy cliffs had protected the Island for 30 years. Now the frustrated sightseers felt that with a new owner the previous rules were relaxed. John Bonham Christie requested voluntary help from Poole solicitors, Messrs Dickinson Manser & Co, and immediately Hugh Green and Kim Parkyn indicated that they would assist at weekends. They started what became Brownsea Island Voluntary Wardens (BIVW), which is still in existence and has grown to about 100 volunteers. Initially the School House was their base. Others assisting in 1961 included Scouts and Wildfowlers. Hugh Green and Kim Parkyn found that boat patrols in their own dinghies were the most effective way to find and to keep off intruders. Barry Guest remembers that the Island was so overgrown that the Bullnose Morris could only just negotiate the circular route along Middle Street to the Vinery, known later as Rocket Corner for some reason, up through Beech Valley and back to the Quay passing the Daffodil Field.

Eventually the Island was offered for sale by tender by Cooper and Tanner Limited of Frome. Offers of over £200,000 were invited. As well as excluding the Church and Churchyard owned by the Church authorities, the Villano was to be retained by John Bonham Christie. Potential purchasers made soundings of likely planning approvals. In discussions locally the possibility of earmarking an area around the two lakes as a Nature Reserve were suggested if other developments were allowed on the Island. Locally there was a hope that the National Trust, the Nature Conservancy or a similar organisation would purchase the Island. Many of the local residents were keen to get access as well as preventing any developments. None of the national bodies had funds to purchase the Island and to maintain it. Local appeals were started. Max Nicholson of the Nature Conservancy and Eddie Shackleton, a naturalist and a director of the John Lewis Partnership, were approached.

When no acceptable offer was made for the Island, the Treasury agreed to consider the Island, valued by them at £110,000, in lieu of death duties. The family were to retain the Villano, its grounds, access to the quay and the use of services (e.g. water, sanitation, etc) available on the Island. The Treasury would accept the Island only if the National Trust would take on the ownership. Normally the National Trust would only accept a property if there was an endowment to cover costs at least for the first few years, and a figure of £100,000 was indicated. Immediately an appeal was made. The organisers included Helen Brotherton, Jack Rathbone, Leslie Miller and solicitor Maurice Yeatman. £10,000 - a good sum in the early 1960s - was raised in one week. Mrs Bonham Christie's wishes were to be carried out but with the provision of visitor access, and it was stipulated in Hansard that there was to be a nature reserve. The National Trust saw the Castle, which had been gutted by fire in 1896, as too much of a liability and of less interest to visitors who would come to the Island, and would not accept the Island unless another organisation took responsibility for the Castle. The John Lewis Partnership agreed to take a lease of the Castle as one of their holiday centres for employees – known as partners – and retired employees. The John Lewis Partnership, the Pilgrim and Dulverton Trusts, the Scout and Guide Association, Dorset Naturalists' Trust (later renamed the Dorset Wildlife Trust) and the Dorset Wildfowlers were amongst the organisations, together with many local residents, who supported the appeal. This enabled the National Trust to accept the Island in 1962. Between then and May 1963, when the Island was officially opened to the public, volunteer wardens were asked to continue their patrols to stop unauthorised landings.

In 1962 the National Trust organisation was quite small. John Gaze was the area National Trust Agent. Alan Bromby who was the Warden on Round Island and previously was the Warden on Furzey Island and had served in the Royal Navy during the war was appointed National Trust Warden for Brownsea Island. Miss Brotherton welcomed this appointment as Alan Bromby knew the islands and had a great interest in the harbour wildlife. The Dorset Naturalists' Trust leased over one third of the Island to manage as a reserve with restricted public access. The DNT had limited funds and their first Warden had half the Villa rent-free. The conditions were poor e.g. no electricity, but Mr and Mrs Walton stayed about three years. Barry Guest who was thinking of returning to a career at sea agreed to remain on the Island with the National Trust as boatman and Assistant Warden. Jack Battrick – who later told his story in 'Brownsea Islander' – had been born on the Island and had left soon after Mrs Bonham Christie bought the Island, returned as an Assistant Warden. This team had a year to prepare the Island for the influx of visitors.

The Island 'jungle' had to be opened up. As well as paths, firebreaks had to be cut. This continued after 1963. With safety in mind the ruined cottages at Maryland were demolished – by the Royal Marines. A zigzag path from the viewpoint at Barnes Top down the cliffs to the South Shore was cut out by a detachment of Territorials, and these steps were named Terrier Steps. Some assistance was not so helpful. A group of Borstal inmates and two Warders did quite a lot of clearing for a week. The second group was not so co-operative and escaped one night. They stole a boat and before they reached Sandbanks they damaged other boats. One boat was John Christie's 'Diligence of Marston'.

Mosquitoes had been breeding freely on the Island for 30 years. The National Trust was worried that the presence – and bite – of mosquitoes would discourage visitors. Poisoning their breeding grounds was not an option. Clearing the undergrowth disturbed them and seemed to make them more active. One builder, Derek Cartridge, claimed that the mosquitoes nearly stopped the transfer of the Island to the National Trust. The builders, erecting scaffolding prior to renovating the exterior of the castle were badly bitten by mosquitoes, and threatened to dismantle the partly assembled scaffolding and to leave the Island. If the Castle was not renovated the John Lewis Partnership might not have taken on the lease of the Castle and the National Trust would not have accepted the Island with full responsibility for the Castle! Luckily the Nature Conservancy Council appointed a scientist (Mr M W Service) to study the problem of mosquitoes in Poole Harbour and especially on Brownsea Island. His study was extended from one to three years. British Drug Houses (BDH), based in West Quay Road, Poole, supplied all the materials for the laboratory set up in a room next to the kitchen in the Villa. Andrew Hawkes, who now owns his family's shoe shop in Poole High Street, but was then a teenager, assisted in the research. Thirty two species of mosquitoes were found on the Island, but only four of the species bit humans. Also many of the mosquitoes bred on Studland. By draining some of the shallow-water breeding

One of the 200 Red Squirrels and seldom seen Sika Deer.

grounds the mosquitoes became less of a problem and now they do not worry the visitors. However it must be remembered that mosquitoes would have a place in the food chain!

As might be expected there is little evidence of numbers of species of birds on Brownsea Island during Mrs Bonham Christie's ownership. A few local ornithologists would look over the sea wall, and one, a Mr Gooch, was allowed on the Island a few times. In the booklet 'Birds of Brownsea' (published by the Dorset Naturalists' Trust) heron nest counts range from 91 nests in 1952 to 35 in 1961. Herons need tall trees to make their nests but other than this the reduction in numbers is probably due to circumstances beyond Mrs Bonham Christie's control.

Red squirrels could be seen on the mainland in the 1950s and 1960s and were not considered to be under threat at that time. On the Island John Manning and Barry Guest saw few. Derek Loader remembers seeing just one and it was dead! The small number sighted could be explained by the lack of open spaces and their movements in the undergrowth could not be observed. In 1963 newspapers reported a small colony of red squirrels. Sika deer introduced to Brownsea Island in the late 19th century had swum to the mainland and can now be found in the wild as far north as the Midlands. Many people are surprised to learn that they can swim. At low tide the water is quite shallow on the south side of the Island and they are able to wade for quite a distance and reach Arne, perhaps via another island. In the 1934 fire most, if not all of the deer were either killed or managed to swim away to safety. However they have returned! With deer on the Island young trees are eaten and natural tree regeneration is impossible without fencing. Wild rabbits had been seen on the Island prior to 1962. In 1962 only a tame rabbit, accompanied by a Golden Pheasant, was noticed. From time to time there are considerable numbers of wild rabbits possibly bred from the survivors of myxomatosis.

Leaving management to Nature, as Mrs Bonham Christie did, can lead to an imbalance or a complete loss of certain species. Intervention by Man can cause unforeseen problems, as with the introduction of Sika deer and rhododendrons in the 19th century. Two pairs of Canada Geese were brought to the Harbour from Yorkshire by Dorset Wildfowlers in the mid 20th century; very few residents welcome the large number of Canada Geese which breed in this area now, despite efforts to control numbers by egg pricking where the nests can be found. On the positive side – in my opinion – young ducklings of mallard and shelduck have been taken from their nests on the Reserve and reared in a brooder. They were released when able to fly. Previously over 80% of these ducklings were being taken by Herring Gulls. Details of the changes and management aims of the Dorset Naturalist Trust (now the Dorset Wildlife Trust) can be found elsewhere. St Andrew's Bay, the mudflats walled in 1853 and drained to make more pasture land, was allowed to flood to form the present Lagoon, with pumps to control the level of water. Islands have been built on the Lagoon, and the Reserve reed beds and marshland are managed to attract various species of birds and insects. Rhododendrons, which stop the light getting to smaller plants and do not support insect life, are being cleared. Regeneration of trees and plants are encouraged. As one of the few colonies of red squirrels remaining in the U.K. special consideration is given to long term planning for tree growth to produce sufficient food for them. In 2001 research scientists estimated that the colony of red squirrels is over 200. Conditions elsewhere – for instance the use of pesticides or the shooting of migrating birds – affect the numbers of birds coming to the Island. Unusual weather patterns or storms create conditions which cannot be foreseen.

The National Trust opened the Island to the public on the 16th May 1963. Lady Olave Baden-Powell, chief of the world-wide Girl Guide Movement and widow of the founder of the Scout Movement, performed the opening ceremony. Tributes were made to the contributors to the Trust Fund needed by the National Trust before they could accept the Island. The 1934 fire had been a warning of serious damage that could be done to wildlife. Three weeks after the opening the worst fears were realised. There was a serious fire on the south side of the Island. Luckily it was dealt with quickly. With so many visitors around them John Bonham Christie and his family found the Villano had lost its old appeal, and he transferred it to the Scout and Guide Association. Later the National Trust exchanged it for South Lodge, which was nearer to the Scout and Guide campsite. The National Trust uses the Villano as a shop and café and remodelled the reception area.

This Chapter gives a brief sketch of Brownsea Island after Mrs Bonham Christie's 34 years of ownership. A naturalist speaking on the BBC at the time of her death paid the tribute 'One of the first conservationists to leave things to Nature. She had left us a little piece of England that has not gone anywhere for 30 years'. The National Trust staff and volunteers have endeavoured to limit the conflict between Man and Nature so that from April until October 100,000 visitors can enjoy Brownsea Island. I leave the reader to decide if Mrs Bonham Christie was the 'Saviour of Brownsea Island'.

Facsimile Letters
from
Mrs Bonham Christie

1-1

February 18 1955

My dear Mrs Loader,

I am writing very late to thank you for the most delicious Pears and oranges you so kindly sent me by your son last Saturday, I have tried each evening to get this letter written to you but I have had so many letters that had to be replied to those I term business letters, several were about my small house at Sandbanks, as some fresh people are going in next week at least Mrs King is, but her husband is in hospital at present, he has been 30 years in charge of the Parkstone

1-2

Cemetery at least it is at Parkstone but Poole who love to claim every thing call it their Cemetery & as he is 61 & ill & not expected to be able to do hard work again they have pensioned him off, but he has to move out of the house they gave him while in their service, she seems a very nice sensible & capable woman she is 59 next month, so I think will be much better than Mrs Lister who has not long left, as she was a hopeless shopper & only liked to do needlework, you see no shop delivers here, so milk, bread, groceries etc. in fact every thing has to go there & my boatman fetches them from there three times a week.

The oranges & Pears were simply perfect & such large fine oranges, I think it is wonderful such lovely fruit & such cold horrid weather, again many, many thanks

Yours sincerely Mary B Christie

Letter to Mrs Loader informing her of the new resident at Brownsea House on the mainland – February 1955.

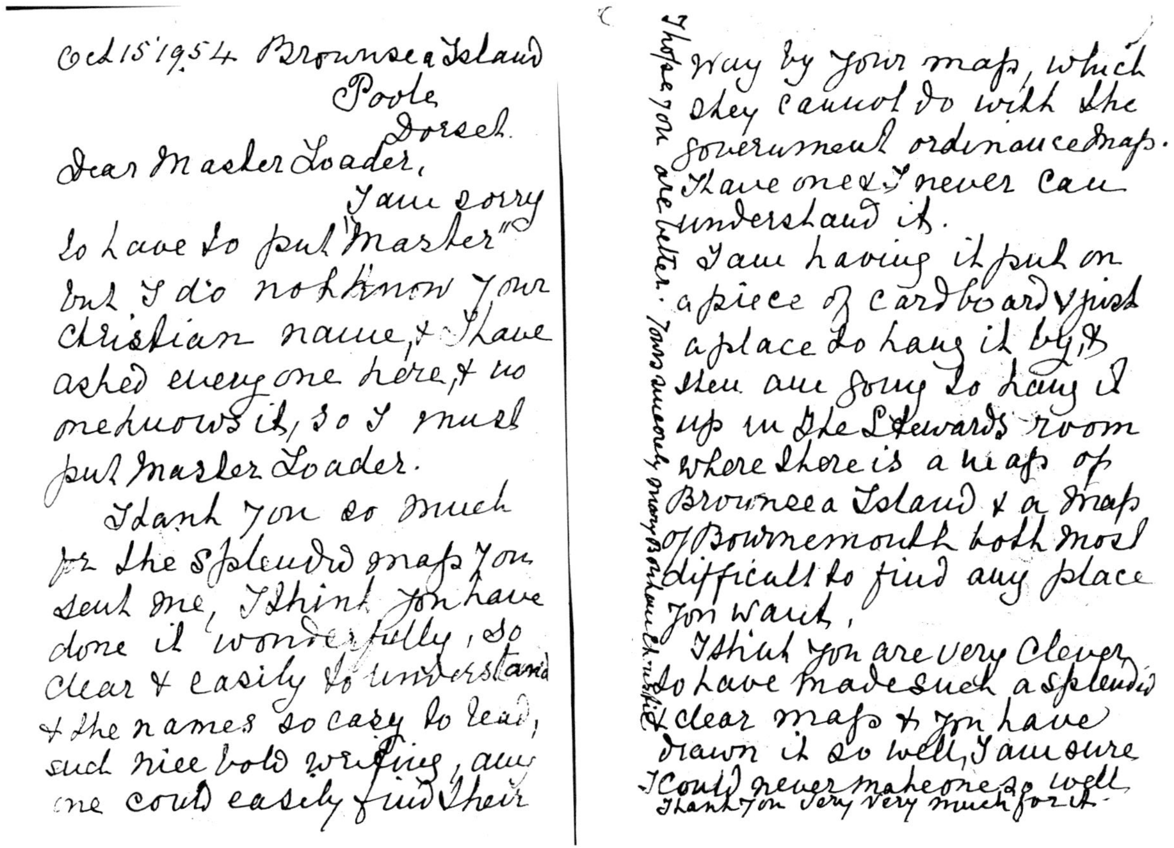
Oct 15' 1954 Brownsea Island
Poole
Dorset.
Dear Master Loader,
I am sorry to have to put "Master" but I do not know your Christian name, & I have asked everyone here, & no one knows it, so I must put Master Loader.
I thank you so much for the splendid map you sent me, I think you have done it wonderfully, so clear & easily to understand & the names so easy to read, such nice bold writing, any one could easily find their way by your map, which they cannot do with the government ordnance map. I have one & I never can understand it.
I am having it put on a piece of cardboard & just a place to hang it by, & then am going to hang it up in the Stewards room where there is a map of Brownsea Island & a map of Bournemouth both most difficult to find any place you want.
I think you are very clever to have made such a splendid & clear map & you have drawn it so well, I am sure I could never make one so well. Thank you very very much for it.
I hope you are better. Yours sincerely Mary Bonham Christie

Letter to Derek Loader who had produced a simplified map of the island – 15 October 1954.

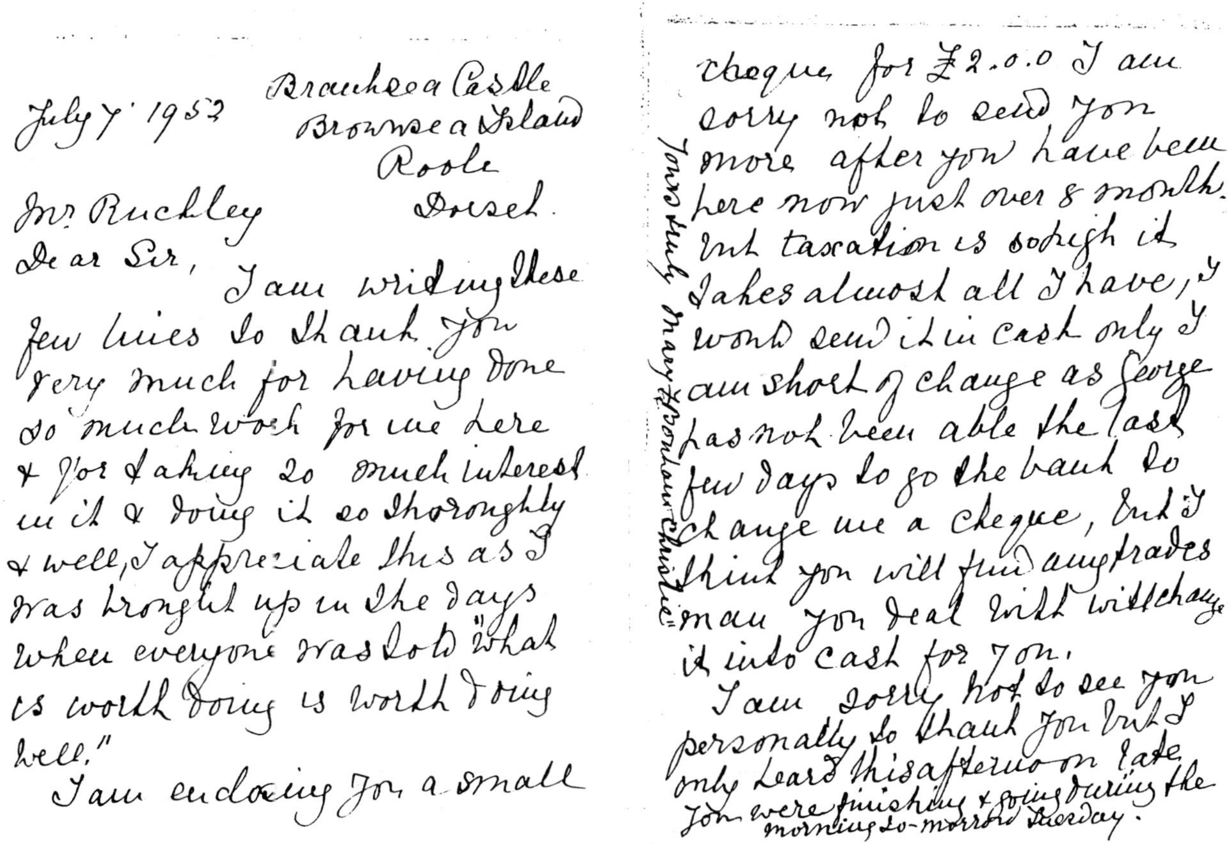

July 7' 1952 Branksea Castle
Brownsea Island
Poole
Dorset.

Mr Buckley

Dear Sir,

I am writing these few lines to thank you very much for having done so much work for me here & for taking so much interest in it & doing it so thoroughly & well, I appreciate this as I was brought up in the days when everyone was told "What is worth doing is worth doing well."

I am enclosing you a small cheque for £2.0.0 I am sorry not to send you more after you have been here now just over 8 months. but taxation is so high it takes almost all I have, I would send it in cash only I am short of change as George has not been able the last few days to go the bank to change me a cheque, but I think you will find any trades man you deal with will change it into cash for you.

I am sorry not to see you personally to thank you but I only heard this afternoon late you were finishing & going during the morning to-morrow Tuesday.

Yours truly Mary F. Bonham Christie"

Mrs Bonham Christie's life long concern about tax is evident in this letter - 1952.

Acknowledgments

This book is the result of 18 months' research. As the majority of the book is based on interviews, I am most grateful to everyone who has discussed their memories of the Island and Mrs Bonham Christie, and allowed me to copy letters and photographs. I have been encouraged and helped by Brownsea Island National Trust staff and volunteers. A brief note of the information used is given below.

Robert Bonham-Christie - great grandson – family cuttings

Property Manager and Personal Assistant, **Barry and Maureen Guest** – cuttings, letters (**Harry Moyle, Mr Murray**) and audiotapes (**Mrs Clara Douie**).

Barry Guest was the Island boatman prior to National Trust ownership

John Barker. Much of Chapter 4 is based on the information he collected from John Anderton, Charles Howell, "Lofty" Ould, Alf Keeping, and Barney Chapman

Kim Parkyn MBE and the late **Beryl Parkyn** – cuttings, cine film (to video), audiotapes (including **Mrs Lou Brayley** – neé Campbell).

Hugh Green – cine film (to video)

Dot Cooke – cuttings, daffodil picking

Bill Parsons – Apprentice plumber

Penny Trent and Judy Cosser, daughters of Gerry Luff – letters, photographs

Helen Brotherton CBE – Wildlife, National Trust ownership

Derek Cartridge – stonemason/bricklayer

'Chappie' and Phyllis Chapman – photographs, cuttings, unpublished 'Toms Story' (Chappie's mother's maiden name was Toms).

Mrs Effamy, late husband, Fred, landed in 1930's

Bernard Seviour, Nigel Patchett, John Wellman, Susan Goodricke, Tony Gardiner – landed in 1950's

Andrew Hawkes – assisted with mosquito research

Miss Blackmore, daffodil picker 1950's – photograph

Mrs Shinn, grandfather worked on the Island

Sally, Norman and Rachel Fawcus (neé Norman), grandchildren of Charles Cooper.

Derek Loader – he, parents and grandfather worked on the Island

Peter Barleycorn, on Island World War II and later visited – photographs, letter

John (Hugh) Manning, worked on the Island 1957 – 1960 – photographs, cuttings

John Bugler, co-author with Gregory Drew of 'Edwardian Brownsea Island' (unpublished) and 'A History of Brownsea Island'

Leonard Martin – born on the Island

Mrs Stooks daughter-in-law of Mr and Mrs Capel – photographs

Mr Futcher, diver

Maurice Cartridge, son of skipper of Mrs Christie's son's yacht

John England, World War II, decoys at Arne

Mrs Farrant, friend of Battrick family – cuttings

Martin Papworth, National Trust Wessex Regional Archaeologist

Late **Harry Moyle** – letters

Brian Woolgar – Scouts/Guides

Unpublished Dean Family Story (1840-1927) by the late **William Dean**

Iris Gray (neé Dingley) – mother knew Mrs Bonham Christie at Southbourne

Mrs Eileen Parr – photo

Mrs Irene Turk (nee Dunford) – refugees

Mr Buckley – letter

Late **Harry Radford** – photo and information from slidea

Mrs Margaret Allen – photos, information

Peter Miles – Rolls Royce "Brownsea"

Ron Worthington – photos and cuttings

Sue Sieger – photos

Ian Andrews – photos

Martin Blyth – photos

Poole Historical Trust – photo (Bristowe Collection)

In addition background reading at Poole Local Studies Centre at the Waterfront Museum, and at Dorset County Museum, Dorchester

Considerable assistance has also been given by:

John Argent and **Alan Marsh** who started the present archive collection on Brownsea Island for the National Trust, and for indexing. Alan has collected details of census returns, marriage registers etc of most of the inhabitants from 1841.

Sheila Argent my typist without whose help my research would not have progressed.

Jean my wife, who has encouraged me, from "What are you doing in your spare time this winter?" to "We must spend a day together this week".

INDEX